William Cobbett's
RURAL RIDES REVISITED

For my Parents

William Cobbett's
RURAL RIDES REVISITED

A Photographic Exploration

by
Laurence Vulliamy

I would especially like to thank Jane and Philip Dunn for their constant encouragement and advice during the preparation of this book; I would also like to thank my designer, Richard Beales, for many hours of sympathetic attention.

Thanks and acknowledgements are due to the following: John Burke, for sharing with me his love of Romney Marsh, Geoff Woodcock, for providing me with many maps from his large collection, Mick Dunn and Barry Harmer for their help with photographic details, The National Trust, and finally all those who stopped and chatted and from whom I gleaned a great deal of local information.

All maps are based on the Ordnance Survey Series and reproduced by sanction of The Controller, Her Majesty's Stationery Office. Crown copyright reserved.

Laurence Vulliamy
June 1977.

First published in Great Britain in 1977.
PIERROT PUBLISHING LIMITED
17 Oakley Road,
London N.1. 3LL.

Hard cover ISBN 0 905310 08 X
Soft cover ISBN 0 905310 03 9

Book design by Richard Beales, Juniper Studios
Typesetting by Saildean in Century Schoolbook 10pt & 9pt.
Photo-repro by Brentwood Lithographic Limited.
Printed and bound by Balding & Mansell Ltd.

Distributed by Wildwood House, 29 King Street, London W.C.1.

Introduction

In 1830, William Cobbett, farmer, journalist, political agitator and anti-establishmentarian, published his collection of 'Rural Rides'. These were a selection of tours made on horseback between 1821 and 1826 throughout the south-east of England that appeared at regular intervals in the 'Weekly Political Register', his own newspaper.

His intentions were to find out the true state of affairs of a country whose landscape was changing as a result of agricultural enclosure and whose growing towns were being swept up in the tide of the Industrial Revolution.

Although he was largely concerned with the welfare of the farming communities, his descriptions of villages, country lanes, fields, pastures and woodlands have never been matched. He wrote down whatever came into his head and although full of digressions his writing leaves us with a spontaneous and emotional account of what he saw.

It is my intention, in this book, to retrace three of his journeys from his earlier rides, and to see just how the now endangered English countryside has changed since Cobbett's time, over one hundred and fifty years ago.

The three 'Rides' that I have chosen to follow cover a cross-section of the area known as 'Cobbett country'. Two he made on horseback and the third, 'The Huntingdon Journal', was made by stage-coach. This was published in a further collection of 'Rides' in 1853 by his son.

He was accompanied by his son on the ride from his seed farm in Kensington to Hurstbourne Tarrant in Hampshire. This place Cobbett insists on calling 'Uphusband', being, he maintained, the correct name. For the Kentish journey I have taken the liberty of joining him halfway through his ride from Worth in Sussex (1823) to Dover and then carrying on as far as Faversham, on the north coast of Kent. This was one journey for Cobbett which, in all, took him nine days to reach London. For the sake of publication he made it into two separate 'Rides'.

The use of photographs in this book will enable the reader to make a comparison with Cobbett's original descriptions and see what changes have inadvertently occurred.

A book cannot provide the senses of sound and smell so vital to the enjoyment of the open air. I hope that with the use of occasional map references from the Ordnance Survey Grid the reader will feel it is possible to go out and find the original English countryside.

Throughout the book William Cobbett's narrative appears in the smaller typeface.

William Cobbett

William Cobbett was born at Farnham in Surrey on the 9th of March 1763, the son of a farmer, the landlord of 'The Jolly Farmer', a pub which now bears his name. He started his working life early as a human scarecrow in a blue smock; later he was allowed to reap and plough. He had no formal education, only that which he managed to pick up from his father. At the age of twenty he became a clerk to a Gray's Inn attorney before joining the army. He served in Canada for six years, latterly as a sergeant-major. It was during this time that he first encountered the corruption that was rife in the services; he returned with distinction but had to flee to France with his new wife to escape a court-martial, having exposed some of his late officers.

WILLIAM COBBETT
A contemporary engraving – (reproduced by kind permission of Mr. Robert Thornton)

The next eight years he spent in America, teaching English to French refugees in Philadelphia and as 'Peter Porcupine' writing fierce attacks on Tom Paine and the native Democrats. Twice he was prosecuted for libel and in 1800 he returned to England. The then Tory government gave him a hero's welcome and offered him the editorship of the government newspaper. This he declined, but in 1802 he began to publish his famous 'Weekly Political Register' which, with one three month break in 1817, continued until his death. Though Tory at first it gradually changed its politics until it became the champion of the Radical cause.

Cobbett settled at Botley in Hampshire where he farmed. This was probably the happiest time of his life, as shown in his writings. However the government were becoming increasingly embarrassed with his attacks on the corruption of public life and Cobbett spent two years (1810-1812) in Newgate for criminal libel. Fearing a second prison sentence and the threat of bankruptcy, he returned to America in 1817.

Having farmed on Long Island, he came back to England two years later and stood for Parliament, but failed to be elected. He began his Rides in 1821; these included lecture-tours and meetings with the farmers up and down the country. He was tried for sedition in 1830. This was the year of the great rising of agricultural labourers which saw rick burning and the smashing of machinery in south-east England. His acquittal and triumph over the government brought him great fame as the champion of the workers' cause, though he went to great pains to discourage the acts of violence.

In 1832 he was returned as Member of Parliament for Oldham. This was the Reformed Parliament for which he had, for so long, campaigned. On 18th June 1835, he died at Normandy Farm near Guildford and was buried at Farnham. He was the author of over fifty works as well as the originator of Hansard.

Contents

Kensington to Uphusband

through the counties of Middlesex, Surrey and Hampshire.

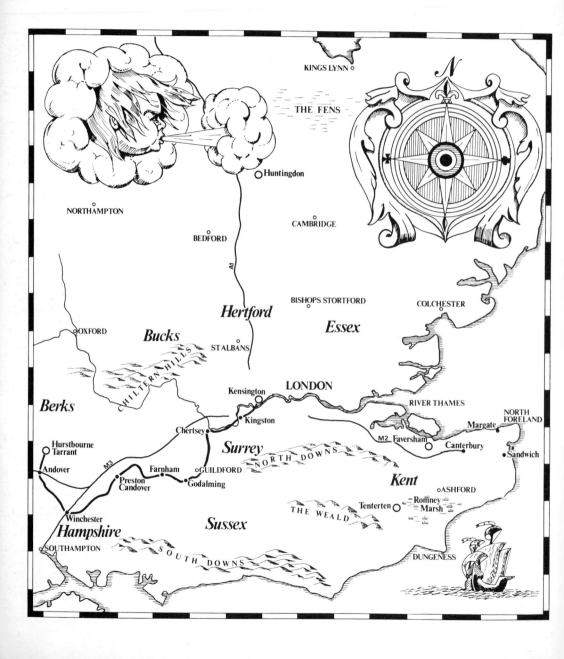

I can rarely walk along a towpath without half-expecting to be flattened by a person on a bicycle, dressed like one of 'The Temperance Seven', travelling at great velocity, and trying to keep up with the sleek eight on the river alongside him. Under the shadow of Hammersmith Bridge, on the Barnes peninsular, there is a notice which says: 'No person is allowed to ride or drive any horse or drive any cart, wagon or other vehicle or ride, wheel or in any way use any bicycle or tricycle over or upon any part of the towpath. By order.' It appears that with the possible exception of boat race days, The Port of London Authority actually realises the potential of their towpaths. It is a lovely walk too; from one side round to Putney Bridge and in the other direction along to Barnes Bridge past playing fields and through trees and gardens.

The road to Barnes Common passes the 'Boileau' pub, known locally as 'The Boiler' and along Castlenau with its share of private hotels, hardly 'freequarter'. The Common approached from Rocks Lane appears to be just a wooded throughfare but away from the roads, down some of the paths, it becomes very countrified. Vine Road on the west side has two rural level crossings with some grassy clearings between the belts of trees. While walking around I was closely watched by three squirrels that I could see and,

Chilworth, Near Guildford, Surrey.
Wednesday, 25th Sept. 1822.
This morning I set off, in rather a drizzing rain, from Kensington, on horseback, accompanied by my son,(James), with intention of going to Uphusband, near Andover, which is situated in the north-west corner of Hampshire ... **My object was, not to see inns and turnpike-roads,** but to see the *country;* to see the farmers at home, and to see the labourers in the fields; and to do this you must go either on foot or on horseback ... **All Middlesex is** *ugly,* notwithstanding the millions upon millions which it is continually sucking up from the rest of the kingdom; and, though the Thames and its meadows now and then are seen from the road, the country is not less ugly from Richmond to Chertsey-bridge, through Twickenham, Hampton, Sunbury and Sheperton, than it is elsewhere. The soil is a gravel at bottom with a black loam at top near the Thames; further back it is a sort of spewy gravel; and the buildings consist generally of tax-eaters' showy, tea-garden-like boxes, and of shabby dwellings of labouring people who, in this part of the country, look to be about half *Saint Giles's:* dirty, and have every appearance of drinking gin.

BELOW HAMMERSMITH BRIDGE

judging by the rustlings, a few more that I couldn't see. Following the A306, the road climbs up through Roehampton to meet the A3 on Putney Heath. I was soon on the Kingston bypass, leaving behind me places with names such as New Malden, Berrylands and Norbiton. Esher was the next labelled bit of suburbia. The approach road, with Sandown Park Racecourse on the right and Little-worth Common, was considerably more encouraging than the strings of brick boxes with mock-tudor shop fronts and a proliferation of off-licences that I had just come through. The people of Esher are building houses fast and swallowing up the wooded slopes of Claremont Park once the home of Sir John Vanbrugh, the architect. It is an odd thing, and certainly it seems peculiar to this part of residential Surrey, that so many streets are marked 'Private Road, Residents Only' or 'Access to Residents Only', in a display of the human territorial instinct.

Leaving Esher on the A224 it was not long before I crossed the river Mole. The Esher Road runs alongside. Turning off at the roundabout onto the old Esher Road, the view is lovely across the meadows as the river meanders away to meet the Thames at East Molesley. Standing on the bank with my back to the housing estate it was as if I was deep in the country.

RIVER MOLE NEAR ESHER

BARNES COMMON

ST. ANNE'S HILL

Joining the A317 the road passes briefly beside Walton Common before approaching Weybridge. Here the roads are lined with beautiful beech trees which obscure much of the surrounding buildings. It can be a surprise, when climbing a tree-lined hill in this area, to reach the top and find yourself in built-up suburbia again. Chertsey lies on the other side of Weybridge and, still on the A317 and through the main town, the turning up to St. Anne's Hill, the B388, can be found. The actual turning into the drive by the lodge is very easy to miss as there is only a very small sign on the gate. Once inside, the path carries you up onto the hill which is covered with beech trees and rhododendrons and holly. Once again I was being watched by a rustling squirrel community although considerably more discreet than their contemporaries on Barnes Common; I managed a conversation with one who greeted me with a kind of barking noise which I returned to the best of my ability. On the far side of the hill the path ends at the inevitable leafy bower where the view stretches over the Shepperton plains and reservoirs to Heathrow Airport; the aeroplanes can be seen silently taking off in rapid succession. Immediately below and out of sight, the roar of the traffic along the M3 compensates for the lack of aircraft noise.

At Chertsey, where we came into Surrey again, there was a fair for horses, cattle and pigs. I did not see any sheep. Everything was exceedingly *dull* ...

This county of Surrey presents to the eye of the traveller a greater contrast than any other county in England. It has some of the very best and some of the worst lands, not only in England, but in the world. We were here upon those of latter description. For five miles on the road towards Guildford the land is a rascally common covered with poor heath, except where the gravel is so near the top as not to suffer even the heath to grow. Here we entered the enclosed lands, which have the gravel at bottom, but a nice light, black mould at top; in which the trees grow very well. Through bye-lanes and bridle-ways we came out into the London road, between Ripley and Guildford, and immediately crossing that road, came on towards a village called Merrow ...

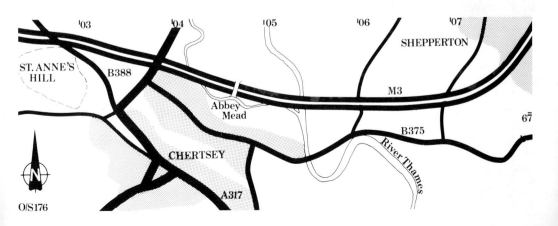

Turning back through Chertsey it was reassuring to find a little of the parochial atmosphere that once characterised a place many miles from London. Today, along with Weybridge and Byfleet, they have all become part of the 'Wen' in its ceaseless spread. Matthew Arnold wrote: "Chertsey, the stillest of country towns, leads nowhere but to the heaths and pines of Surrey". That is hardly true today.

One of the most pleasant places in Weybridge is around the old river bridge out of the town and along the River Wey marshes. Parts of this belong to the National Trust, as do the banks of the River Wey Navigation, running upstream. Needless to say the old bridge is overshadowed by a new wide-arched bridge, but the interesting lock and weir are in a pleasant grassy area. There are boatyards nearby, in the summer this is probably a place to be avoided if you care little for crowds.

HAM LOCK

THE OLD BRIDGE, WEYBRIDGE
RIVER & MARSHES, HAM MOOR

The road to Byfleet, the B374, runs through the back of Weybridge and past the railway station. Opposite is a road up a wooded hill called 'Cobbett's Hill, The Heath'. The B374 carries on through some very expensive suburbia and to the left is St. George's Hill, an Iron Age encampment. Today this is perhaps the most exclusive residential area in Surrey. It has been the home of three of The Beatles and many other celebrities of stage and screen; all credit must go to the ancients for their good taste in real estate.

Just through West Byfleet, the A245 crosses the River Wey Navigation. There are footpaths running beside the river, which looks in need of dredging at this point. It would be generous to say that meadows run along both sides, nevertheless there are some green fields and some fine trees. It is not long before Upshot Lane turns off to the left. The signpost is marked Ripley. Here, in the last throes of the 'Wen', a country lane is recognisable amongst the houses along by a sign marking the end of the speed restriction. The road turns and sinks and I drove between hedges of hawthorn and ripening blackberries, with mud on the road from the thick tyres of a tractor. I could see a clear view over the open countryside from a small lay-by where a stile gave me extra height. The road takes a turn down a small hill into Pyrford. This is a delightful place with a farm, first on your left, then some cottages with the Norman church across the road looking out over the broad meadows of the River Wey. Inside the church is a rare Norman fresco, painted in 1140, the date of the building. It was only uncovered when the more recent picture painted over it was being restored.

The meadows lie below Pyrford and the road falls quite steeply down onto the level. Here was the open space and fresh air that I had been looking for. The road and river are both lined with willows; it must be a fine sight during flood. Two footpaths, one from the first bridge you come to, the other from the pub, run across the flats away to the south-west and Old Woking. To the east are the ruins of Newark Priory. Sadly the eastern aspect is spoilt by the line of pylons running behind the ruins. The river breaks into three streams across the level and there is an interesting weir above the weather-boarded mill that stands in grandeur over the main stream. In a small copse of trees opposite the weir are the remains of an older weir in the undergrowth. There are some pleasure boats moored upstream, most of which seem to have incongruous names. Downstream the river flows away to the Royal Horticultural Society's gardens at Wisley.

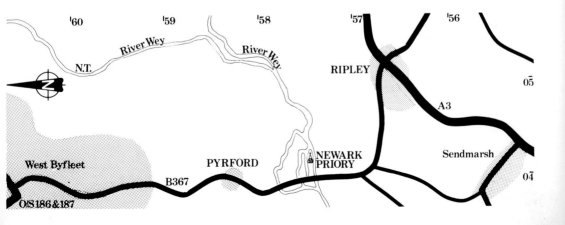

12

PYRFORD MEADOWS

Ripley has withstood, for so long, the rush and rumble of the main A3 traffic which bisects the village. Today Ripley has never been so quiet, thanks to the bypass which has saved Ripley but, in doing so, has considerably changed the outlying countryside. At the turn of the century the village was a Mecca for cyclists as it was surrounded by attractive country and within easy reach of the metropolis. In fact the Gamages catalogue of 1899 lists cycling shoes; along with the 'Holborn' and the 'North Road' it has the 'Ripley'. People came to watch the cricket matches on the huge and beautiful village green which Arthur Mee described as "a cradle of cricket".

South of the A3 and through a small market place runs the lane to West Horsley. I passed through a very long avenue of beech trees a short way out of Ripley, having crossed over the new road. The farms on either side of the road have some tidy fields but few hedges. The soil here is a thicker gault, compared with the rich alluvial soil of the Wey vale. Joining the A246 at West Horsley, I drove in the direction of Guildford, past Hatchlands, a National Trust property containing the first known decorative work by Robert Adam, and into East Clandon. To the south of the road the fields rise away to the woods on top of the North Downs. The Pilgrims' Way runs along the other side of the ridge on its way to Canterbury. I turned up into West Clandon, having driven around a one way road for a mile or so. Here I found the 'Onslow Arms', the local pub. The landlord told me that the pub used to be a hostelry for the labourers working on the Clandon Park estate, owned by the Onslow family. A gateway to the house was not far away. Only the house and garden belong to the Trust, bequeathed in 1956. The present Earl lives at nearby Temple Court, surrounded by the private parkland of the original estate. The park, laid out by Capability Brown,

Lord Onslow lives near Merrow. This is the man that was, for many years, so famous as a driver of four-in-hand. He used to be called *Tommy Onslow*. He has the character of being a very good landlord. I know he called me "a d—d *Jacobin*" several years ago, only, I presume, because I was labouring to preserve to him the means of still driving four-in-hand, while he, and others like him, and their yeomanry cavalry, were working as hard to defeat my wishes and endeavours ...

THE GATES CLANDON PARK

GILLRAY'S CARICATURE OF THOMAS, 1ST EARL OF ONSLOW
(Reproduced by kind permission of the National Trust)

stretches from the huge iron gates on the main road just outside Merrow to embrace most of the parish of West Clandon. There is a footpath running right through the estate to the village on the far side. Even in Cobbett's day this was a heavily populated area. The chalk downs of Merrow were very popular for horse riding and racing. There were many great houses in the neighbourhood then; besides Clandon there were Effingham Hall, Horsley Towers, and Fetcham and Eastwick Parks. Most of these have now become schools or training establishments. With the coming of the railway to the Downs, the commuter invaded. Now the descendants of the estate workers, domestics, gardeners and agricultural workers all flock to the same trains wearing the same clothes and returning to the same houses with such names as 'Fernden' and 'The Oaks'. What countryside remains is remarkably free of power lines and rubbish tips.

MISTLETOE CLANDON PARK

FROM NEWLANDS CORNER

CLANDON PARK

Newlands Corner is described by the Surrey County Council as 'Open Space', and there are signs up to tell you if you had not already realised. There is a car park and 'facilities area' nearby for people to come and sit in their cars. More to the point, there is one of the most beautiful views in Surrey if not in the South of England. It was over this steep ridge of chalk that Cobbett clambered on his way to St. Martha's Hill, and he remarks on the view. Sidney Allnutt's poem, first published in the 'Spectator' in 1907, captured its essence:

> Far southward from St Martha's Hill
> and to the east and west,
> The downs heave up great shoulders, till
> The distance with its magic blue
> Envelops every other hue,
> And crest is lost in crest.

The sandy rise of St. Martha's Hill, I am told, is clearly visible from the ridge and it can be found along Guildford Lane, a turning off the A248 through Albury. A car park is provided at the foot of the hill, reached along a most beautiful country lane, at once narrow and tree-lined, then open as it passes paddocks and small fields. The gateways give provocative glimpses of neat and well-tended farm buildings. St. Martha's Hill is another 'Open Space'. The chapel on the summit is approached up a steep sandy hillside covered with rough bracken and heather. For one of the most barren and wind-swept places it is not lonely. It is directly on The Pilgrims' Way; this was the track used in the Middle Ages by pilgrims who travelled to Thomas Becket's shrine at Canterbury. The track, dating from 800 BC, follows a contour above the base of the chalk and today is part of the newly established footpath, that runs from Farnham through Surrey and Kent, called the North Downs Way.

BELOW ST. MARTHA'S HILL

'02   '03   '04   '05   '06

To Guilford

Newlands Corner

4̄9

A25

ST. MARTHA'S HILL

Pilgrim's Way

Silent pool

River Tillingbourne

A248

Albury

4̄8

N

CHILWORTH MILLS

O/S186&187

To come to Chilworth, which lies on the south side of St. Martha's Hill, most people would have gone along the level road to Guildford, and come round through Shawford under the hills; but we, having seen enough of streets and turnpikes, took across over Merrow Down, where the Guildford racecourse is, and then mounted the "Surrey Hills," so famous for the prospects they afford. Here we looked back over Middlesex, and into Buckinghamshire and Berkshire, away towards the north-west, into Essex and Kent towards the east, over part of Sussex to the south, and over part of Hampshire to the west and south-west. We are here upon a bed of chalk, where the downs always afford good sheep food. We steered for St. Martha's Chapel, and went round at the foot of the lofty hill on which it stands. This brought us down the side of a steep hill, and along a bridle-way, into the narrow and exquisitely beautiful vale of Chilworth, where we were to stop for the night. This vale is skirted partly by woodlands and partly by sides of hills tilled as corn fields. The land is excellent, particularly towards the bottom. Even the arable fields are in some places, towards their tops, nearly as steep as the roof of a tiled house; and where the ground is covered with woods the ground is still more steep. Down the middle of the vale there is a series of ponds, or small *lakes,* which meet your eye, here and there, through the trees.

ST. MARTHA'S CHAPEL

I was leaning over a gate a short way from Chilworth Manor when I met George Parrott who has been farming in the area for the past twenty five years. He works five hundred acres, a lot for the area, but was saying that the land, has been over-farmed and the soil is very tired. He blames the fertilisers that are put down in great abundance. Leaf-mould, he maintains, is the answer. Organic farming should be encouraged and with proper rotation the fields would return to peak productivity.

Down Halfpenny Lane towards Chilworth is the river Tillingbourne. Here by the bridge are the ruins of the Chilworth Powder Mills. The river has diminished somewhat by the lowering of the water-table but still flows briskly over the crags and falls of the valley bed. As I walked into the woods by West Lodge, the waterfall sounds came to my ear at different pitches and from different directions. Then further along the path, the noise became louder until I came across the central area where the main mills once stood. There are huge stones lying around the bases of the trees, some completely overgrown with ivy. The air seemed sweet here. The edge of the wood is clearly defined; where the trees stop, the modern bungalows begin. The main street through Chilworth is a progression of dreadful half-timbered modern bungalows, with the equally uninspiring name, 'Southern Bungalows'. Save for a few old houses there is barely anything left of beauty in the vale that Cobbett described so enthusiastically.

Through Chilworth I took the B2128 to Wonersh and then on to Godalming over some open meadows by Peasmarsh Lock, on the River Wey again. The road bends and twists along a bank lined with willow trees before it joins the main A3100 into Godalming. The river meanders through the. town and the open greens lend a 'Constable-eye-view' to the town's aspect.

Here are some very fine farms, a little strip of meadows, some hop-gardens, and the lakes have given rise to the establishment of powder-mills and paper- mills. The trees of all sorts grow well here; and coppices yield poles for the hop-gardens and wood to make charcoal for the powder-mills.

They are sowing wheat here, and the land, owing to the fine summer that we have had, is in a very fine state. The rain, too, which, yesterday, fell here in great abundance, has been just in time to make a really good wheat-sowing season. The turnips all the way that we have come, are good. Rather backward in some places; but in sufficient quantity upon the ground, and there is yet a good while for them to grow. All the fall fruit is excellent, and in great abundance. The grapes are as good as those raised under glass. The apples are much richer than in ordinary years. The crop of hops has been very fine here, as well as everywhere else. The crop not only large, but good quality. They expect to get *six* pounds a hundred for them at Weyhill Fair ...

THE CHILWORTH MILLS

(THE POWDER MILLS)

The East India Company set up mills in this area in 1625. It is possible some mills existed earlier. Gunpowder and, later, cordite were produced. Manufacture ceased after the 1914-1918 war.

Explosions took place and in the one in 1917 many people died.

Little more than foundations may be seen but there are mill stones and waterways which were formed for transport and power to drive the wheels and turbines.

Bank notes were produced in the reign of Queen Anne and it is likely some of the mills were used for this purpose.

Cobbett referred to a fine crop of hops here in 1822, and to the narrow and exquisitely beautiful vale of Chilworth. The Chilworth Powder Mills "goaded him to fury".

Lea, Near Godalming, Surrey,
Thursday, 26 Sept.

We started from Chilworth this morning, came down the vale, left the village of Shawford to our right, and that of Wonersh to our left, and crossing the river Wey, got into the turnpike-road between Guildford and Godalming, went on through Godalming, and got to Lea, which lies to the northeast snugly under Hing-Head, about 11 o'clock. This was coming only about eight miles, a sort of rest after the 32 miles of the day before …

We got into free-quarter again at Lea; and there is nothing like free-quarter, as soldiers well know. Lea is situated on the edge of that immense heath which sweeps down from the summit of Hind-Head, across to the north over innumerable hills of minor altitude and of an infinite variety of shapes towards Farnham, to the northeast, towards the Hog's Back, leading from Farnham to Guildford, and to the east, or nearly so, towards Godalming. Nevertheless, the inclosed lands at Lea are very good and singularly beautiful. The timber of all sorts grows well; the land is light, and being free from stones, very pleasant to work. If you go southward from Lea about a mile you get down into what is called, in the old Acts of Parliament, the *Weald* of Surrey. Here the land is a stiff tenacious loam at top with blue and yellow clay beneath. This weald continues on eastward, and gets into Sussex near East Grinstead: thence it winds about under the hills, into Kent. Here the oak grows finer than in any part of England. The trees are more spiral in their form. They grow much faster than upon any other land. Yet the timber must be better; for, in some of the Acts of Queen Elizabeth's reign, it is provided that the oak for the royal navy shall come out of the Wealds of Surrey, Sussex, or Kent.

TILFORD BRIDGE

Odiham, Hampshire,
Friday, 27 Sept.
From Lea we set off this morning about six o'clock to get free-quarter again at a worthy old friend's at this nice little plain market-town. Our direct road was right over the heath through Tilford to Farnham; but we veered a little to the left after we came to Tilford, at which place on the green we stopped to look at an *oak tree*, which, when I was a little boy, was but a very little tree, comparatively, and which is now, take it altogether, by far the finest tree that I ever saw in my life. The stem or shaft is short; that is to say, it is short before you come to the first limbs; but it is full *thirty feet round,* at about eight or ten feet from the ground. Out of the stem there come not less than fifteen or sixteen limbs, many of which are from five to ten feet round, and each of which would, in fact, be considered a decent stick of timber. I am not judge enough of timber to say anything about the quantity in the whole tree, but my son stepped the ground, and as nearly as we could judge, the diameter of the extent of the branches was upwards of ninety feet, which would make a circumference of about three hundred feet. The tree is in full growth at this moment. There is a little hole in one of the limbs; but with that exception, there appears not the smallest sign of decay.

At this point I took the liberty of disgressing from Cobbett's route; rather than following the A3 trunk-road through Milford to Hindhead and then double back again to Tilford, I decided to take the B3001 roughly following the Wey valley. It must be noted though that the area around Hindhead provides some spectacular views especially from the top of Gibbett Hill, 895 feet above sea-level. This is wild country which Cobbet did not like, presumably because it was not productive; he described Hindhead in a separate ride as "certainly the most villainous spot that God ever made". An acacia tree was planted on the small green at Thursley in commemoration of Cobbett.

Away from the fumes and roar of the A3, the other side of Milford, the B3001 opens out to flat arable land with fields bordered by tall trees. Elstead has a fine village green and a Post Office in the front room of somebody's house. The road continues over a stone bridge with five arches, typical of the bridges in this part of the valley. Two more can be found at the little village of Tilford, to the west. Here stands the King's Oak that Cobbett calls "by far the finest tree that I ever saw in my life". It measures 26 feet around the girth; it has been severely pruned, of necessity, and there are some unsightly pieces of metal covering the stumps. Dotted around the village green are oak trees that have been planted to commemorate various coronations and royal jubilees. The two branches of the river Wey join here, one coming from Farnham and the other from beyond the Frensham Ponds.

TILFORD

BRITISH OAK
PLANTED TO COMMEMORATE
THE 60 YEARS REIGN OF
QUEEN VICTORIA
1897

THE TILFORD OAK

WAVERLEY ABBEY

MEADOWS NEAR WAVERLEY ABBEY

The B3001 continues towards Farnham, through some beautiful beech woods and the sort of terrain that reminds me of Buckinghamshire. As the road takes a sharp left hand turn it meets the river again at a delightful spot by a bridge with some old cottages nearby. Just opposite the bridge is a turning and the wood opens out into the lowland, with sight of the ruins of Waverley Abbey. This is now under the care of the Ministry of Public Buildings and Works. The grand house now overlooking it, some call it Waverley Abbey, is now an old people's home. It has an ornamental lake in front with a small bridge to enhance the perspective. The cows roam over the pastures and the ducks roam over the lawns. The ruins are overshadowed by the house, but despite Ministry involvement, nature reigns; an old yew stands by the high altar, a splendid beech in the south transept spreads its branches over the walls of the chapter house and an ash tree commands what was once the treasury.

Waverley Lane, to Farnham, follows the Wey valley. Nearby is Moor Park, now a college; it was the seat of Sir William Temple for whom Jonathan Swift worked as a secretary. It was here that Swift wrote his satires 'The Battle of the Books' and 'The Tale of a Tub', the latter William Cobbett admits to being the foundation of his own literary interests.

The tree has made great shoots in all parts of it this last summer and spring; and there are no appearances of *white* upon the trunk, such as are regarded as the symptoms of full growth. There are many sorts of oak in England; two very distinct; one with a pale leaf, and one with a dark leaf: this is of the pale leaf The tree stands upon Tilford-green, the soil of which is a light loam with a hard sand stone a good way beneath, and, probably, clay beneath that. The spot where the tree stands is about a hundred and twenty feet from the edge of a little river, and the ground on which it stands may be about ten feet higher than the bed of that river.

In quitting Tilford we came on to the land belonging to Waverly Abbey, and then, instead of going on to the town of Farnham, veered away to the left towards Wrecklesham, in order to cross the Farnham and Alton turnpike-road, and to come on by the side of Crondall to Odiham. We went a little out of the way to go to a place called the *Bourn,* which lies in the heath at about a mile from Farnham. It is a winding narrow valley, down which, during the wet season of the year, there runs a stream beginning at the *Holt Forest,* and emptying itself into the *Wey* just below Moor-Park, which was the seat of Sir William Temple when Swift was residing with him. We went to this bourn in order that I might show my son the spot where I received the rudiments of my education.

WAVERLEY HOUSE
WAVERLEY LANE

Farnham was the birthplace of Cobbett and in the churchyard lies his grave. The pub in which he was born was called 'The Jolly Farmer'; only recently has it been called 'The William Cobbett'. It stands by the side of the river, opposite the church, on the corner of a now busy main road out of Farnham, the A287. Just below the bridge over a very small River Wey is a bronze bust of the great man looking out, over what must have been grazing pastures, towards the town.

Further out of town along the A287, the road takes a steep dive down into the Bourne valley. Here is a sand-hill, probably the one Cobbett rolled down with his friends in his youth. The church stands on the edge of the steep valley with the slope immediately below it. Now the hop-garden Cobbett mentions is no more than another suburban dead-end street. The stream still runs with a footpath beside it which leads to the church and around the back of the houses via Oldchurch Lane.

There is a little hop-garden in which I used to work when from eight to ten years old; from which I have scores of times run to follow the hounds, leaving the hoe to do the best it could to destroy the weeds; but the most interesting thing was a *sand-hill,* which goes from a part of the heath down to the rivulet. As a due mixture of pleasure with toil, I with two brothers, used occasionally to *desport* ourselves, as the lawyers call it, at this sand-hill. Our diversion was this: we used to go to the top of the hill, which was steeper than the roof of a house; one used to draw his arms out of the sleeves of his smock-frock, and lay himself down with his arms by his sides; and then the others, one at head and the other at feet, sent him rolling down the hill like a barrel or a log of wood. By the time he got to the bottom, his hair, eyes, ears, nose, and mouth were all full of this loose sand; then the others took their turn, and at every roll there was a monstrous spell of laughter. I had often told my sons of this while they were very little, and I now took one of them to see the spot. But that was not all. This was the spot where I was receiving my *education;* and this was the sort of education; and I am perfectly satisfied that if I had not received such an education, or something very much like it; that, if I had been brought up a milksop, with a nursery-maid everlastingly at my heels, I should have been at this day as great a fool, as inefficient a mortal, as any of those frivolous idiots that are turned out

COBBETT'S BIRTHPLACE – A CONTEMPORARY ENGRAVING

from Winchester and Westminster School, or from any of those dens of dunces called colleges and universities. It is impossible to say how much I owe to that sand-hill; and I went to return it my thanks for the ability which it probably gave me to be one of the greatest terrors, to one of the greatest and most powerful bodies of knaves and fools that ever were permitted to afflict this or any other country.

From the Bourne we proceeded on to Wrecklesham, at the end of which we crossed what is called the river Wey. Here we found a parcel of labourers at parish-work. Amongst them was an old playmate of mine. The account they gave of their situation was very dismal. The harvest was over early. The hop-picking is now over; and now they are employed *by the parish;* that is to say, not absolutely digging holes one day and filling them up the next; but at the expense of half-ruined farmers and tradesmen and landlords, to break stones into very small pieces to make nice smooth roads lest the jolting, in going along them, should create bile in the stomach of the over-fed tax-eaters ...

We left these poor fellows, after having given them, not "religious tracts," which would, if they could, make the labourer content with half starvation, but something to get them some bread and cheese and beer, being firmly convinced that it is the body that wants filling and not the mind. However, in speaking of their low wages, I

To reach Wrecklesham, I had to go back up the hill and turn off the road to the left onto the B3384. This takes you past Upper Bourne. At the foot of School Hill there is a turning into Greenfield Road and here there is a small cul-de-sac called Cobbett's Way. It is a dismal dead-end of white houses. I would have thought that the Urban District Council could have found a slightly more appropriate spot to name after the town's most famous son.

Back on the Wrecklesham Road I turned into River Lane, which in true character crosses the river and then crosses the main A31 road to Alton. The road becomes Runwick Lane as it climbs the side of the valley past Runwick House and Ridgeway House. Looking back into the vale, Farnham lies between the hills, the tip of a fearful conglomeration of Aldershot, Farnborough, Camberley and Bagshot.

From the gaps in the hedges the ploughed fields spread away; just past Grover's Farm you cross from Surrey into Hampshire. Part of the fun of travelling down these country lanes is the possibility of taking the wrong turning. Cobbett mentions his route over Slade Heath, which is not marked on the current Ordnance Survey Map but is clearly marked on the First Editions. Today the road runs over what was once this heathland, a high level of chalk with a belt of trees on the east side, now enclosed and ploughed fields. Through the gaps in the trees you can see the unmistakable twin humps of Horsedown Common.

told them that the farmers and hop-planters were as much objects of compassion as themselves, which they acknowledged.

We immediately, after this, crossed the road, and went on towards Crondall upon a soil that soon became stiff loam and flint at top with a bed of chalk beneath. We did not go to Crondall; but kept along over Slade Heath, and through a very pretty place called Well. We arrived at Odiham about half after eleven, at the end of a beautiful ride of about seventeen miles, in a very fine and pleasant day.

HORSEDOWN COMMON

WELL, THE CROSSROADS

The road drops considerably before coming into Well. It is as if you have stepped into a different time; there is the nucleus of graceful houses and barns, with a pub and, of course, a well on the main crossroads. Horsedown Common can be reached from a little track out of the village on the Crondall Road. However, passing through the village, the lane to Odiham is the next left turning to the north. The land here levelled out considerably as I approached Odiham, coming off the chalk bed and onto the sandy clay.

Called "the most attractive town in the county", Odiham is still the "nice little plain market town" that Cobbett described. Once the home of small farmers, seed merchants, corn merchants and traders, the buildings reflect the prosperity of the past. The fine church stands above a small square called 'The Bury' (there are stocks and whipping-post in the churchyard) and timber-framed houses with irregular roofs contrast with the elegant, porched houses of the High Street.

ODIHAM

The chalky land begins again along the lanes to Upton Grey. The road rises and falls as do the fields, often with trees at the crests of the hills. There are many ditches, some sprouting willow trees, presumably self-sown. The lane runs almost straight through Upton Grey and Weston Patrick, crossing the main A339 Basingstoke to Alton road before starting to wind through the chalk hills towards Preston Candover. After the main road it becomes Bagmore Lane and then Axford Road. This is another true country lane. Its direction is governed by the level of the terrain; lined mostly with beech trees, it skirts the steep grey hillsides, providing a different view around every corner. As you look up, often you can see a hillside outlined with a proud set of ash trees which, as Cobbett said, "always grows well upon the chalk". The fields of thick loam are speckled with huge flints. I asked at a farm on the road and one of the workers said that there is no problem cultivating the fields; barley, wheat and linseed grow on the open, sloping hillsides, uninterrupted by pylons or telegraph poles.

TO UPTON GREY

OLD MAN'S BEARD

WATTLING

Winchester,
Saturday, 28th Sept.
Just after day-light we
started for this place. By the
turnpike we could have come
through Basingstoke by turning
off to the right, or through
Alton and Alresford by turning
off to the left. Being naturally
disposed towards a middle
course, we chose to wind down
through Upton-Gray, Preston-
Candover, Chilton-Candover,
Brown-Candover, then down to
Ovington, and into Winchester
by the north entrance. From
Wrecklesham to Winchester we
have come over roads and lanes
of flint and chalk. The weather
being dry again, the ground
under you, as solid as iron,
makes a great rattling with the
horses' feet. The country where
the soil is stiff loam upon chalk,
is never bad for corn. Not rich,
but never poor. There is at no
time anything deserving to be
called dirt in the roads. The
buildings last a long time, from
the absence of fogs and also the
absence of humidity in the
ground. The absence of dirt
makes the people habitually
cleanly; and all along through
this country the people appear
in general to be very neat. It is a
country for sheep, which are
always sound and good upon
this iron soil. The trees grow
well, where there are trees. The
woods and coppices are not
numerous; but they are good,
particularly the ash, which always grows well upon the chalk.
The oaks, though they do not
grow in the spiral form, as upon
the clays, are by no means
stunted; and some of them very
fine trees; I take it, that they
require a much greater number

PRESTON CANDOVER   VIEW TOWARD BECKETTS DOWN

Preston Candover is the largest of the Candovers. The B3046 that runs through the villages is the 'scenic route' from Basingstoke to Winchester. There are some fine houses in Preston Candover including some beautiful thatches. To the west, on the hilltop, runs a line of Scotch pines, not to be confused with the avenue of yew trees that Cobbett admired, which are to be found at the other side of the next village, Chilton Candover. The local butcher at Preston Candover, Mr Osgood, a keen rambler, suggested that the trees were part of an ancient Saxon parish boundary. It is also worth noting that the avenue also runs adjacent to a line running between two Roman sites, suggesting a track or road. Or of years to bring them to perfection than in the *Wealds*. The wood, perhaps, may be harder; but I have heard that the oak, which grows upon these hard bottoms, is very frequently what the carpenters call *shaky*. The underwoods here consist, almost entirely, of hazel, which is very fine, and much tougher and more durable than that which grows on soils with a moist bottom. This hazel is a thing of great utility here. It furnishes rods wherewith to make fences; but its principal use is to make *wattles* for the folding of sheep in the fields. These things are made much more neatly here than in the south of Hampshire and in Sussex, or in any other part that I have seen. Chalk is the favourite soil of the *yew-tree;* and at Preston-Candover there is an avenue of yew-trees, probably a mile long, each tree containing, as nearly as I can guess, from twelve to twenty feet of timber, which, as the reader knows, implies a tree of considerable size. They have probably been a century or two in growing; but, in any way that timber can be used, the timber of the yew will last, perhaps, ten times as long as the timber of any other tree that we grow in England.

ST. MARY'S, PRESTON CANDOVER

PRESTON CANDOVER

CHILTON CANDOVER

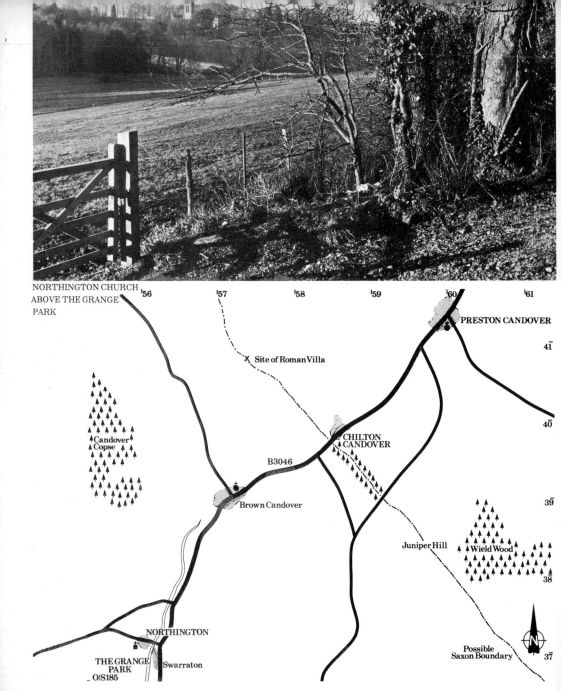

NORTHINGTON CHURCH
ABOVE THE GRANGE
PARK

|56 |57 |58 |59 |60 |61

PRESTON CANDOVER

4$\bar{1}$

X Site of Roman Villa

4$\bar{0}$

Candover
Copse

CHILTON
CANDOVER

B3046

Brown Candover

3$\bar{9}$

Juniper Hill

Wield Wood

38

NORTHINGTON

THE GRANGE
PARK
O/S185   Swarraton

Possible
Saxon Boundary

3$\bar{7}$

N

perhaps they were planted as a drive or boundary for a house, now demolished.

At Northington, the Grange, once the home of the Baring family, is now derelict. The Grange Park still exists and from the road the little river can be seen running through the meadows around to the big lake behind the trees. In Northington Church, built by the squire in 1890, lie the graves of his family, the Barings; they lie at the west side of the churchyard whilst the villagers lie to the east. There are still descendants living in the area. On the flower rota pinned inside the church porch, one of the names was a Miss Baring. The churchyard is damp, mossy and mysterious.

Quitting the Candovers, we came along between the two estates of the two Barings. Sir Thomas, who has supplanted the Duke of Bedford, was to our right, while Alexander, who has supplanted Lord Northington, was on our left. The latter has enclosed, as a sort of outwork to his park, a pretty little down called Northington Down, in which he has planted, here and there, a clump of trees. But Mr. Baring, not reflecting that woods are not like funds, to be made at a heat, has planted his trees *too large;* so that they are covered with moss, are dying at the top, and are literally growing downward instead of upward. In short, this enclosure and plantation have totally destroyed the beauty of this part of the estate. The down, which was before very beautiful, and formed a sort of *glacis* up to the park pales, is now a marred, ragged, ugly-looking thing. The dying trees, which have been planted long enough for you not to perceive that they have been planted, excite the idea of sterility in the soil. They do injustice to it; for, as a down, it was excellent. Everything that has been done here is to the injury of the estate, and discovers a most shocking want of taste in the projector. Sir Thomas's plantations, or rather those of his father, have been managed more judiciously …

On the road to the Alresfords, Abbotstone Down is a popular picnic place; there are footpaths from here to Winchester and to the Candovers.

Just before Broad Street meets the main A31 Winchester Road at New Alresford, it runs along the top of a bank that dams up the Old Alresford Pond, heavily populated with wild birds. Beyond the other side of the road flows the River Alre, a good twenty feet below. Here it runs through the terraces of a watercress farm.

The B3047 turns off the A31, signposted to King's Worthy. The first lane to the left takes you down to Ovington. This lane is a wonderful introduction to a magical place. It is very narrow and as it disappeared into the trees I was confronted with a little ford and a very narrow bridge. Having negotiated these I then found myself in the yard of a watermill. The road bends around the house and away over the main bridge over the River Itchen. I spoke to a fisherman on the bridge who told me, with a certain amount of pride, that the river contained nothing but trout, apart from the wise old pike which they had been after for years. "He'll eat his own weight of trout in a week" the fisherman said, with tacit admiration. The river runs very fast in a shallow gravel bed with weed and watercress growing along the banks. Willow trees stand on the banks shading the horses who drink from the swirling water. A perfect English setting. I watched a yellow wagtail for about fifteen minutes bustling around the water's edge rooting out its food. The main part of the village stands up the hill on drier ground. A short way up this hill there is a turning to the right which leads back towards the river. This road follows the contour of the valley, looking down on the meandering stream, and is lined with some very old trees. In one field I saw some sheep with extremely long fleeces, looking as if they hadn't been sheared for two seasons.

A WATERCRESS SLUICE

TO OVINGTON

THE RIVER ITCHEN AT OVINGTON

WINCHESTER CATHEDRAL
THE WEST FRONT

THE WHITE SWAN

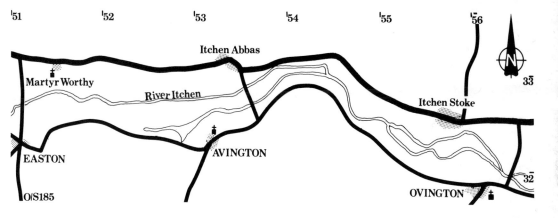

Along the valley both Avington and Easton are beautiful villages. The former has a classic Georgian church in good condition; the path from the road to the church door is paved with grave stones. Easton has some very old cottages and a splendid whitewashed plaster and timber-framed barn which, along with the cottages, is thatched in characteristic Hampshire style.

The approach to Winchester is ugly. Inevitable trading estates and faceless houses do nothing for what was once the beautiful Itchen valley. It is uncertain just where Cobbett's dinner with the farmers was on the night that he delivered his 'Rustic Harangue'. He mentions going to 'The Swan Inn' but at the time there was 'The Black Swan' or 'The White Swan'. Today the 'Black Swan Buildings' are not the original and are Inland Revenue offices; it would please Cobbett to think that the place had fallen to 'The Thing', Cobbett's disparaging name for the Establishment. Outside the old North Wall, in Hyde Street, stands 'The White Swan' which is most likely to have been the place. The landlord has an old list of licensees dating back to the time the place was opened in the 1740's, and a later list of some of the 'events'. It includes large meetings and dinners for local societies.

Winchester,
Sunday morning, 29 Sept.
Yesterday was market-day here. Everything cheap and falling instead of rising ... Proceeding upon the true military principle, I looked out for free quarter, which the reader will naturally think difficult for *me* to find in a town containing a *cathedral*. Having done this, I went to the Swan Inn to dine with the farmers. This is the manner that I like best of doing the thing. *Six-Acts* do not, to be sure, prevent us from *dining* together. They do not authorise justices of the peace to kill us, because we meet to dine without their permission ...

I wish to see many people, and to talk to them: and there are a great many people who wish to see and talk to me. What better reason can be given for a man's going about the country and dining at fairs and markets? ...

To avoid the main road I took the B3420, the old turnpike out of Winchester up to Andover. It is an old Roman road running straight through some of the most beautiful expanses of country. The land is chalky outside Winchester again and the hills roll gently away on either side. There are large, neat fields enclosed with thick hedges of yew trees that run for considerable distances acting as windbreaks. The road itself is lined with beech trees, a very pleasant and common sight in this county. The trees are usually planted along a parish boundary and many roads follow these boundaries. This particular boundary turns off to the north east, a short way before the road crosses the A30 and runs round to Sutton Scotney. The land became flatter as I came into the Test valley from the high hills near Newton Down Farm.

Wherwell is a very pretty village. It sits under the chalk ridge on the edge of the river Test which, like the Itchen, is also very fast flowing along a shallow bed. It has many characteristic white-plastered and thatched houses, and a shop called bluntly '20th Century Stores'. At the top of the village is an almost derelict thatched cottage called simply 'Toll Cottage'. By far the most beautiful part of Wherwell (pronounced Hurrell) are the water meadows, once the site of Wherwell Priory. The river often separates into two or three streams throughout its valley and here the meadows are enclosed by water. Above the village the road climbs Red Hill, from where there is a lovely view out over the valley towards Stockbridge, radio telescope and all.

BESIDE THE PRIORY MEADOW, WHERWELL

Uphusband,
Sunday evening, 29 Sept.

We came along the turnpike-road, through Wherwell and Andover, and got to this place about 2 o'clock. This country, except at the village and town just mentioned, is very open, a thinnish soil upon a bed of chalk. Between Winchester and Wherwell we came by some hundreds of acres of ground that was formerly most beautiful down, which was broken up in dear-corn times, and which is now a district of thistles and other weeds. If I had such land as this I would soon make it down again. I would for once (that is to say if I had the money) get it quite clean, prepare it as for sowing turnips, get the turnips if possible, feed them off early, or plough the ground if I got no turnips; sow thick with saintfoin and meadow-grass seeds of all sorts, early in September; let the crop stand till the next July; feed it then slenderly with sheep, and dig up all thistles and rank weeds that might appear; keep feeding it, but not too close, during the summer and the fall; and keep on feeding it for ever after as a down. The saintfoin itself would last for many years; and as it disappeared, its place would be supplied by the grass; that sort which was most congenial to the soil, would at last stifle all other sorts, and the land would become a valuable down as formerly.

I see that some plantations of ash and of hazel have been made along here; but, with great submission to the planters, I think they have gone the wrong way to work, as to the mode of preparing the ground. They have planted *small trees,* and that is right; they have *trenched* the ground, and that is also right; but they have brought the bottom soil to the top; and that is *wrong,* always; and especially where the bottom soil is gravel or chalk, or clay. I know that some people will say that this is a *puff;* and let it pass for that; but if any gentleman that is going to plant trees, will look into my *Book on Gardening,* and into the chapter on *Preparing the Soil,* he will, I think, see how conveniently ground may be trenched without bringing to the top that soil in which the young trees stand so long without making shoots.

This country, though so open, has its beauties. The homesteads in the sheltered bottoms with fine lofty trees about the houses and yards, form a beautiful contrast with the large open fields. The little villages, running straggling along the dells (always with lofty trees and rookeries) are very interesting objects, even in the winter. You feel a sort of satisfaction, when you are out upon the bleak hills yourself, at the thought of the shelter, which is experienced in the dwellings in the valleys.

At this point is is possible to take a choice of route to Hurstbourne Tarrant. The road through Andover has nothing to recommend it at all, whilst the B3048 along the Test valley up through Hurstbourne Priors and St. Mary Bourne is far more attractive. Cobbett travelled through Andover, which today suffers from industrial expansion and a ring road to add to the sprawl. No longer does agriculture alone support the 'neat and solid market town'.

Andover is a neat and solid market town. It is supported entirely by the agriculture around it; and how the makers of *population returns* ever came to think of classing the inhabitants of such a town as this under any other head than that of *"persons employed in agriculture,"* would appear astonishing to any man who did not know those population return makers as well as I do.

RIVER TEST NEAR WHERWELL

COBBETT'S VIEW

37   38   39
To Newbury 54

N

HURSTBOURNE
TARRANT
(Uphusband) 53

A343   B3048

Ancient Field System

O/S185

From Andover it is only a few miles to the top of Hurstbourne Hill, along the A343. From here you can see right down into the steep valley of the Bourne Rivulet and away to the far side. At the bottom of the hill is Hurstbourne Tarrant or, as Cobbett insisted it should be called, Uphusband. It is a 1:7 slope down into the village and it is easy to miss Rookery Farm House, one of the first houses you come to. It is here that William Cobbett stayed on his many excursions, (there are twenty-nine references to Uphusband throughout the entire 'Rides'), with his friend Joseph Blount, a Catholic philanthropist. The house is a square-faced eighteenth century farmhouse set close to the road. In the front wall is a brick inscribed with Cobbett's initials and dated 1825. It was a mason's custom to get a local notary to lay an incised brick and tip the labourers. On the corner of the drive, by the road, is an old lime tree, the sight of which must have welcomed Cobbett after a hard ride. I was shown inside the house by the owner, Mr Peter Rosser. He showed me the room which had been the farm office where he thinks Cobbett must have caught up on his journal. The room faces west and looks out onto the hillside, with sheep grazing. One or two trees break the distance; Cobbett couldn't have wished for a better place to stay. There is nothing in Mr Rosser's garden that Cobbett might have brought from America that is peculiar to that country, though he is very interested in a tree growing at the end of the barn by the side of the house. It is scented and resembles an Ailanthus; with green flowers, rather like chestnut flowers, with a distinctive liquorice smell. The village spreads out along the roads and probably has changed very little since Cobbett's last visit. In the churchyard Joseph Blount is buried under a yew tree. At the back of the church the slope rises so steeply that it is possible to look down onto the top of the church from the hillside.

The village of Uphusband, the legal name of which is Hurstbourn Tarrant, is, as the readers will recollect, a great favourite with me, not the less so certainly on account of the excellent free-quarter that it affords.

ROOKERY FARMHOUSE

Through Romney Marsh

and along the Kentish Seaboard.

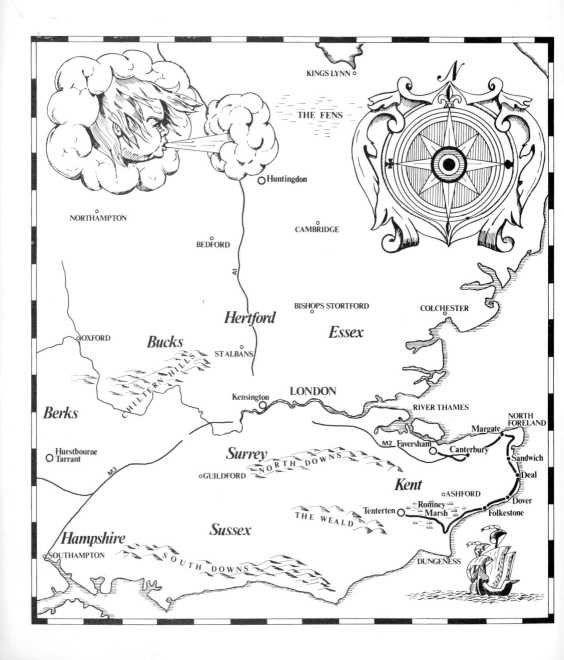

KINGS LYNN

THE FENS

Huntingdon

NORTHAMPTON

BEDFORD

CAMBRIDGE

A1

BISHOPS STORTFORD

COLCHESTER

Hertford

Essex

OXFORD

Bucks

ST ALBANS

C H I L T E R N   H I L L S

LONDON

Kensington

RIVER THAMES

NORTH
FORELAND

Berks

Margate

M2 Faversham

Canterbury

Sandwich

Surrey

N O R T H   D O W N S

Deal

Hurstbourne
Tarrant

M3

GUILDFORD

Kent

ASHFORD

Dover

SOUTHAMPTON

Sussex

THE WEALD

Tenterten

Romney
Marsh

Folkestone

Hampshire

S O U T H   D O W N S

DUNGENESS

From the top of the church tower in Tenterden, I could see down into the fifth quarter of the globe. It is an old saying, immortalised in Kipling's 'Dymchurch Flit' from 'Puck of Pook's Hill', that the world is divided into five continents: Europe, Asia, Africa, America and Romney Marsh. On a clear day it is possible to see the coast of France from the tower, and ships in the Channel use it as a landmark. Tenterden stands over the Marsh like a castle; the lower village of Appledore is the gateway, standing by the moat which corresponds to the Royal Military Canal that runs around the perimeter of the Marsh.

I had climbed the tower of St. Mildred's Church, half expecting to brush past some shrivelled bell-ringer, to catch the view, and to see the layout of the town, which has not changed radically since Cobbett's time. All the development is discreetly hidden behind the old façade of the High Street, or away along the roads leading out of the town. The line of elegant, white weather-boarded houses in the High Street stand facing, across a wide avenue, small cottages with deep front gardens. It has been described as "the most celebrated street in Kent", and also the most photographed. The "very pretty girls" that Cobbett saw have grown up into an abundance of tweed-skirted ladies with little dogs. It is a town of yeoman-farmers and the prosperity has not faded.

Tenterden, Kent
Sunday 31st August 1823

Just before I got to this place I crossed a bit of *marsh* land, which I found, upon inquiry, is a sort of little branch or spray running out of that immense and famous tract of country called *Romney Marsh,* which, I find, I have to cross to-morrow, in order to get to Dover, along by the sea-side, through Hythe and Folkestone.

This Tenterden is a market town, and a singularly bright spot. It consists of one street, which is, in some places, more, perhaps, than *two hundred feet wide*. On one side of the street the houses have gardens before them, from 20 to 70 feet deep. The town is upon a hill; the afternoon was very fine, and, just as I rose the hill and entered the street, the people had come out of church and were moving along towards their houses. It was a very fine sight. *Shabbily-dressed people do not go to church.* I saw, in short, drawn out before me, the dress and beauty of the town; and a great many very, very pretty girls. I saw; and saw them, too, in their best attire. I remember the girls in the *Pays de Caux,* and, really, I think those of Tenterden resemble them. I do not know why they should not; for, there is the *Pays de Caux,* only *just over the water*; just opposite this very place.

HIGH STREET, TENTERDEN

The church at this place is a very large and fine old building. The tower stands upon a base thirty feet square. Like the church at Goudhurst, it will hold *three thousand* people...

This evening I have been to the Methodist Meeting-house. I was attracted, fairly drawn all down the street, by the *singing*. When I came to the place the parson was got into prayer. His hands were clenched together and held up, his face turned up and back so as to be nearly parallel with the ceiling, and he was bawling away, with his *'do thou,'* and *'mayest thou,'* and *'may we,'* enough to stun one. Noisy, however, as he was, he was unable to fix the attention of a parcel of girls in the gallery, whose eyes were *all over the place*, while his eyes were so devoutly shut up. After a deal of this rigmarole called prayer, came the *preachy*, as the negroes call it; and a *preachy* it really was. Such a mixture of whining cant and of foppish affection. I scarcely ever heard in my life ... Monstrous it is to think that the Clergy of the Church really encourage these roving fanatics. The Church seems aware of its loss of credit and of power. It seems willing to lean even upon these men; who, be it observed, seem on their part, to have taken the Church *under their protection* ...

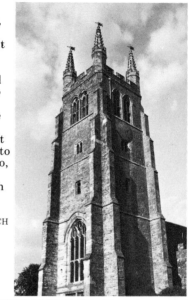

ST. MILDRED'S CHURCH

FOOTPATH TO THE VICARAGE

The most interesting feature of the town is the church-ard. The huge tower stands solidly at one end and at the ther end, along the path from the High Street to the icarage, is a line of windows along the back of the adjoining uilding. Timber-framed and pantiled, the walls lean at all ngles, at one point almost defying the laws of gravity. It is delightfully rustic place tucked away from the rumbling orries and bus queues.

I am indebted to Mr Mason of Bethersden for the ollowing information about the hop-growing industry: vhereas Cobbett remarked that eight tons from ten acres vas "a very great crop", it is not uncommon now to get a on per acre from a high-yield hop. Mr Mason grows two strains of this type called 'Target' and 'Progress', these do iot suffer from 'the wilt', a disease that has, until recently, iearly wiped out Kentish hop-farming. Current market prices are unsteady but whereas a low-yield hop will make

The *hops* about here are *not so very bad*. They say, that one man, near this town, will have *eight tons* of hops upon *ten acres* of land! This is a *great crop any year*: a very great crop. This man may, perhaps, sell his hops for 1,600 pounds! What a *gambling* concern it is! However, such hop-growing always was and always must be. It is a thing of perfect *hazard*.

THE CHURCHYARD

£75 a hundredweight, the high-yield variety makes considerably more, depending on its strength.

From Tenterden the B2080 road falls gently away to the edge of the Marsh. It crosses the Tenterden Sewer which is an undignified word for a drainage river, similar to the 'Leam' in the Fen country. Appledore stands between the Isle of Oxney and the Great Heron Wood. Oxney is barely 200 feet above sea-level but it appears to be much higher, standing at the edge of the vast flats of Romney Marsh. It was an island when the river Rother flowed out to sea at Appledore and beyond towards Old Romney, but a storm in 1287 altered its course drastically. It now flows to the south side of Oxney and out to the sea at Rye.

Folkestone, Kent
Monday noon, 11 Sept.

From Tenterden I set off at five o'clock, and got to Appledore after a most delightful ride, the high land upon my right, and the low land on my left. The fog was so thick and white along some of the low land, that I should have taken it for *water*, if little hills and trees had not risen up through it here and there. Indeed, the view was very much like those which are presented in the deep valleys, near the great rivers in New Brunswick (North America) at the time when the snows melt in the spring, and when, in *sailing* over those valleys, you look down from the side of your canoe, and *see the lofty woods beneath you*! I once went in a log-canoe across a *sylvan sea* of this description, the canoe being paddled by two Yankees. We started in a *stream*; the stream became a wide water, and that water got deeper and deeper, as I could see by the trees (all was woods), till we got to sail amongst *the top branches of the trees*.

FIVE WATERING SEWER, SNARGATE

THE ROYAL MILITARY CANAL NEAR APPLEDORE

To think of shipyards in Appledore is not such a stretch of the imagination; the church that once stood on the edge of a sea creek now watches over the Marsh and the Royal Military Canal. It smells musty inside, as do most of the marshland churches. It can probably seat three hundred people but hardly the three thousand that Cobbett mentions.

I met a man outside the church repairing a wall. His father was a waggoner and used to take people to church from the farms. During the regular floods he would take them through water that was up to the horse's belly. Fairfield Church was the most difficult to reach. It still stands just below Oxney, in the middle of nowhere. Here amongst the drainage dykes, surrounded by grazing sheep and cattle, it is a place peculiar to the Marsh, one of its special places. This man had recently completed some granite work on the sea-wall at Dymchurch. He was very proud of it and he told me to go and have a look if I was passing by the number 23 Martello Tower. He described how to make stonework look old, especially if a wall needed repairing with new stone; he could give it an illusion of age by rubbing fresh cow-dung onto the drying cement, to encourage moss to grow quickly, thus blending new stone with old.

By-and-by we got into a large open space; a piece of water a mile or two, or three or four wide, with *the woods under us!* A fog, with the tops of trees rising through it, is very much like this; and such was the fog that I saw this morning in my ride to Appledore. The church at Appledore is very large. Big enough to hold 3,000 people; and the place does not seem to contain half a thousand old enough to go to church.

In coming along I saw a wheat-rick making, though I hardly think the wheat can be dry under the bonds. The corn is all good here; and I am told they give twelve shillings an acre for reaping wheat.

APPLEDORE –
THE ROAD DOWN TO THE MARSH

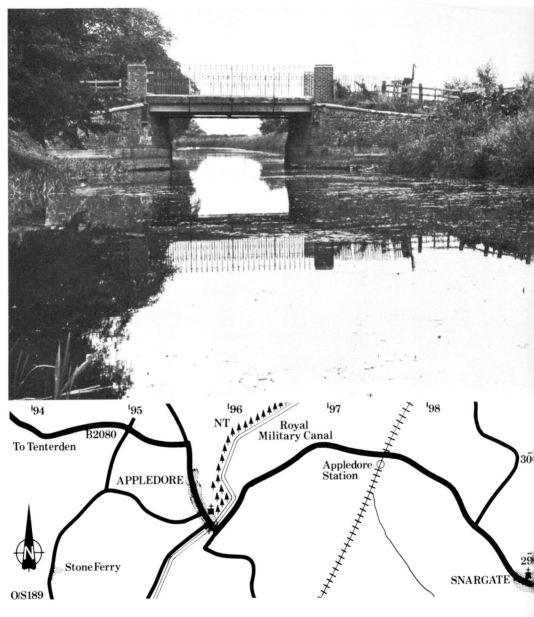

Crossing the canal I followed the road onto the Marsh. Just before the bridge there is a signpost for Rye. Along this lane, which runs along the edge of the canal, the canal can be seen at its best. It was built by William Pitt in 1805 as a defensive measure against the threat of Napoleonic invasion. It runs from the river Rother at Rye, around the perimeter of the Marshes, through Hythe to its outfall at Seabrook. Most of the banks are lined with trees, including the four miles between Appledore and Warehorne owned by The National Trust. The banks provide some lovely walks with the constant accompaniment from the many larks that live on the Marsh.

In quitting this Appledore I crossed *a canal* and entered on *Romney Marsh*. This was *grassland* on both sides of me to a great distance. The *flocks* and *herds* immense. The sheep are of a breed that takes its name from the marsh. They are called *Romney Marsh sheep*. Very pretty and large. The wethers, when fat, weigh about twelve stone; or, one hundred pounds. The faces of these sheep are *white*; and, indeed, the whole sheep is as white as a piece of *writing-paper*. The wool does not look dirty and oily like that of other sheep. The cattle appear to be *all* of the *Sussex* breed. *Red*, loose-limbed, and, they say, a great deal better than the Devonshire.

How curious is the *natural economy* of a country! The *forests* of Sussex; those miserable tracts of heath and fern and bushes and sand, called Ashdown Forest and Saint Leonard's Forest, to which latter Lord Erskine's estate belongs; these wretched tracts and the not much less wretched farms in their neighbourhood, *breed the cattle*, which we see *fatting* in Romney Marsh! They are calved in the spring; they are weaned in a little bit of grassland; they are then put into stubbles and about in the fallows for the first summer; they are brought into the yard to winter on rough hay, peashaulm, or barley-straw; the next two summers they spend in the rough woods or in the forest; the two winters they live on straw; they then pass another summer on the forest or at *work*; and then they come here or go elsewhere to be fatted. With cattle of this kind and with sheep such as I have spoken of before, this Marsh abounds in every part of it; and the sight is most beautiful.

At three miles from Appledore I came through Snargate, a village with *five houses*, and with a church capable of containing *two thousand people!* The *vagabonds* tell us, however, that we have a *wonderful increase of population!* These *vagabonds* will be *hanged* by-and-by, or else justice will have fled from the face of the earth.

At Brenzett (a mile further on) I with great difficulty got a rasher of bacon for breakfast. The few houses that there are, are miserable in the extreme. The church here (only a *mile* from the last) nearly as large; and nobody to go to it. What! will the *vagabonds* attempt to make us believe, that these churches were *built for nothing!* 'Dark ages' indeed those must have been, if these churches were erected without there being any more people than there are now. But, *who* built them? Where did the *means*, where did the hands, come from? This place presents another proof of the truth of my old observation: *rich land* and *poor labourers*. From the window of the house, in which I could scarcely get a rasher of bacon, and not an egg, I saw numberless flocks and herds fatting and the fields loaded with corn!

TO WAREHORNE

THE CHURCHYARD, OLD ROMNEY

The road follows the raised bank of the Roman Rhee Wall which was also the old course of the Rother, dividing Romney Marsh proper from Walland Marsh, south of the road. Snargate is thinly disguised as a small collection of farm buildings, whilst Brenzett is now beset with dull council houses. Brookland is a farming village and here more of the Marsh is under the plough. Old Romney has very little left of what must have been a thriving sea port. The ancient church is set back from the main road in grazing pasture approached from a tree-lined lane by some old farmhouses. Surrounded by sheep, even the churchyard looks as if it is used for grazing. Inside the church the uneven flagstones almost squelch with water and everything smells musty and salty; patches of green damp can be seen invading the whitewash on the walls. Happily, it remains unrestored.

The next village, which was two miles further on, was Old Romney, and along here I had, for great part of the way, cornfields on one side of me and grass-land on the other. I asked what the amount of the crop of wheat would be. They told me better than *five quarters to the acre.* I thought so myself. I have a sample of the *red wheat* and another of the *white.* They are both very fine. They reap the wheat here *nearly two feet from the ground;* and even then they cut it three feet long! I never saw corn like this before. It very far exceeds the corn under Portsdown Hill, that at Gosport, and Titchfield. They have here about eight hundred large, very large, sheaves to an acre ... In a garden here I saw some very fine *onions,* and a prodigious crop; sure sign of most excellent land. At this Old Romney there is a church (two miles only from the last, mind!) fit to contain one thousand five hundred people and there are, for the people of the parish to live in twenty-two, or twenty-three, houses! And yet the *vagabonds* have the impudence to tell us, that the population of England has *vastly increased!* Curious system that *depopulates Romney Marsh* and *peoples Bagshot Heath!* It is an unnatural system. It is the vagabond's system. It is a system that must be destroyed, or that will destroy the country.

OLD ROMNEY CHURCH

From the little lane at the back of the church the road leads to the heart of the Marsh. The main road, bypassing Old Romney church, continues into New Romney, one of the Cinque Ports. Once a prosperous and wealthy borough, it has suffered a diminishing maritime trade and a silting harbour. It is now a market town known more as a station on the Romney, Hythe and Dymchurch Light Railway than as an ancient borough. St. Nicholas church is huge and to its east there is a slight drop in the level of the land where ships used to sail up to the church and moor to rings in the walls. Today there are only modern bungalows and a rubbish dump. The church tower is an important landmark from the Marsh though it has been upstaged by the vast blocks of the Dungeness Power Station. From the town to the beach is about a mile along a suburban street, with an exciting view of the sea through a long avenue of trees. Littlestone-on-Sea remains a respectable Victorian seaside resort, unspoilt by commercial trappings.

The *rotten borough* of New Romney came next in my way; and here, to my great surprise, I found myself upon the sea-beach; for I had not looked at a map of Kent for years, and, perhaps, never. I had got a list of places from a friend in Sussex, whom I asked to give me *a route to Dover*, and to send me through those parts of Kent which he thought would be most interesting to me. Never was I so much surprised as when I saw *a sail*. This place, now that the *squanderings* of the thing are over, is, they say, become miserably poor.

INTERIOR
ST. CLEMENT'S CHURCH
OLD ROMNEY

ST. NICHOLAS, NEW ROMNEY   LITTLESTONE-ON-SEA

ROMNEY MARSH NEAR DYMCHURCH

Instead of taking the main A259 along the coast, I took the B2070 out from the back of New Romney towards Ivychurch. It joins up with the lane from Old Romney into the Marsh. Along the route to St. Mary in the Marsh the horizon is spoiled by the National Grid System of pylons from Dungeness Power Station to the north and south of the Marsh. A little way along the road I found an old sheep-dip that was still in use and had been since 1928 (so the farmer assured me). The road was scattered with sheep-pens and odd enclosures that looked as if they might have been in use for hundreds of years.

The Romney Marsh sheep have changed since Cobbett's time. Because the Marsh is so exposed the sheep have to be very tough to withstand the winds and rain without any shelter. The pure-bred Romney is unsuitable for the meat market yet cross-breeding has led to an animal that can stand up to the exposure of both winter and summer and yet has the right quality of meat and wool. Even so, farmers still run their pure-bred flocks side by side with their half-breeds, since too much cross-breeding is undesirable.

A SHEEP DIP NEAR IVYCHURCH

I came across two men hoeing thistles in a huge field. They were strawberry farmers. Besides all the crops that are grown on the Marsh, which include wheat, oats, linseed, beans, potatoes, sugar beet and maize, farmers from Lincolnshire have begun to grow bulbs. There are seed crops such as spinach, cress, carrots and peas as well as clover. A great deal of the produce is now grown for the 'pick your own' market that thrives in the summer. Certainly strawberries seem to be a good investment, since that was all that these two men grew.

A strange paradox has developed with field drainage; it has been so efficient that the water-table has dropped too low. With the extreme drought this last summer the sluices became dangerously low so that sea water was seeping into the main drains and effectively poisoning the water used for irrigation. Eels were dying in large numbers from lack of water and causing a clearance problem in the dykes.

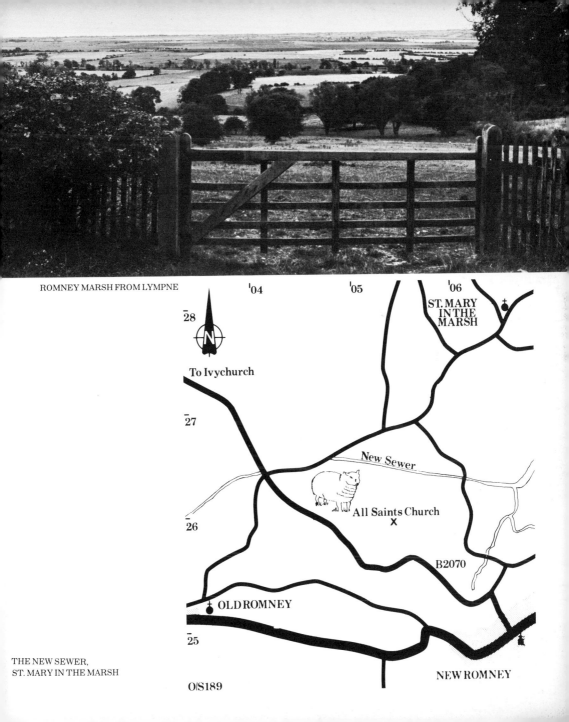

ROMNEY MARSH FROM LYMPNE

'04 '05 '06

ST. MARY
IN THE
MARSH

‾28

To Ivychurch

‾27

New Sewer

All Saints Church
X

‾26

B2070

OLD ROMNEY

‾25

THE NEW SEWER,
ST. MARY IN THE MARSH

O/S189

NEW ROMNEY

At St. Mary in the Marsh the church spire is the familiar landmark again. Here in the churchyard is the grave of Edith Nesbitt, the much loved writer of children's stories, (including 'The Phoenix and the Carpet' and 'The Railway Children'). In her later life she married a retired sea captain, who, on her death, erected over her grave a simple barge-board that he carved himself. There is also a plaque inside the church to her memory. It was while travelling from St. Mary in the Marsh to Dymchurch that I found what I think to be the true spirit of the Marsh. The sun was breaking through an avenue of trees by the side of a dyke with sun-bleached, wind-eroded sheep-pens leaning over in disuse by the side of the water. There was a slight breeze rustling in the reeds, but the atmosphere was made all the more poignant by the songs of the larks as they darted up and down trying to distract me from their nests.

ST. MARY IN THE MARSH

From New Romney to Dimchurch is about four miles, all along I had the sea-beach on my right, and, on my left, sometimes grass-land, and sometimes corn-land. They told me here, and also further back in the Marsh, that they were to have 15*s*. an acre for reaping wheat.

From Dimchurch to Hythe you go on the sea-beach, and nearly the same from Hythe to Sandgate, from which last place you come over the hill to Folkestone. But, let me look back. Here has been the *squandering!* Here has been the *pauper-making work!* Here we see *some of these causes* that are now sending some farmers to the workhouse and driving others to flee the country or to cut their throats!

Dymchurch was the home of the legendary Dr. Syn and the town rather predictably echoes after him. It is not a place of beauty. The approach roads are lined with holiday chalets and the place where I had lunch advertised, 'Restaurant and Antiques', yet the only thing that caught my eye was a plastic bonsai tree. They call it a children's paradise but the beach is dirty and there seems to be little to attract visitors. There are two Martello Towers actually in the town, the northerly one, number 24 in the chain, is now the Martello Tower Museum. The chain of towers were erected between 1805 and 1808 along the South Coast as part of the coastal defences. Originally there were 74 towers but many have decayed and collapsed or been destroyed. They were built either as gun towers or more particularly to defend the marsh sluice-gates. The few that remain are in some cases restored, but more often left to decay, closed against any intrusion. One notable tower on the sea front in Hythe has been converted into a private house.

HYTHE

The road to Hythe follows the towering sea-wall but the development of chalet villages on the other side of the road blight the aspect over the Marsh. Before reaching Hythe there are the Barracks. The beach is sealed off so that no one can walk along it to Hythe and the road into the town is one of the most depressing that I have ever seen, with lines

THE DYMCHURCH SEA WALL

I had baited my horse at New Romney, and was coming jogging along very soberly, now looking at the sea, then looking at the cattle, then the corn, when, my eye, in swinging round, lighted upon a *great round building*, standing upon the beach. I had scarcely had time to think about what it could be, when twenty or thirty others, standing along the coast, caught my eye; and, if any one had been behind me, he might have heard me exclaim, in a voice that made my horse bound, 'The Martello Towers by—!' Oh, Lord! To think that I should be destined to behold these monuments of the wisdom of Pitt and Dundas and Perceval! Good God! Here they are, piles of bricks in a circular form, about three hundred feet *(guess)* circumference at the base, about forty feet high, and about one hundred and fifty feet circumference at the top. There is a door-way, about midway up, in each, and each has two windows. Cannons were to be fired from the top of these things, in order to defend the *country against the French Jacobins!*

I think I have counted along here upwards of thirty of these ridiculous things, which, I dare say, cost *five*, perhaps *ten* thousand pounds each; and one of which was, I am told, *sold* on the coast of Sussex, the other day, for two hundred pounds! There is, they say, a chain of these things all the way to Hastings! I dare say they cost millions. But, far indeed are these from being all, or half, or a quarter of the squanderings along here.

84

Hythe is half *barracks*; the hills are covered with barracks; and barracks most expensive, most squandering, fill up the side of the hill. Here is a Canal (I crossed it at Appledore) made for the length of thirty miles (from Hythe, in Kent, to Rye, in Sussex) to *keep out the French*; for, those armies who had so often crossed the Rhine and the Danube, were to be kept back by a canal, made by Pitt, thirty feet wide at the most! All along the coast there are works of some sort or other; incessant sinks of money; walls of immense dimensions; masses of stone brought and put into piles. Then you see some of the walls and buildings falling down; some that have never been finished. The whole thing, all taken together, looks as if a spell had been, all of a sudden, set upon the workmen; or, in the words of the Scripture, here is the *'desolation of abomination, standing in high places …*

CHURCH HILL, HYTHE

of dull terraces and gravel pits facing the Barracks.

Despite this approach, the town itself is full of character. The church stands on a high cliff with a long walk up Church Hill from the High Street. The Royal Military Canal comes in from the marshes with a very pleasant park area around it in the town. Its exit to the sea is through a sluice, the other side of Hythe at Seabrook. Sadly, the waterway in all its elm-lined glory disappears out of twin sewer pipes into the sea. Similar to New Romney, Hythe is separated from the sea by a Victorian development of some charm. The fishing boats congregate at the western end of the town next to the Martello Towers; the sea-wall runs from this point all the way around to Sandgate Castle. The road along the wall is regularly washed by the sea, threatening the comfortable residences and leaving drifts of sand and seaweed everywhere.

The High Street in Sandgate is full of "nice young men who sell antiques", as Noel Coward wrote. From the high cliffs above Sandgate runs a little toll-road and nearby is Spade House, once the home of H. G. Wells. His house is now a vegetarian boarding house. The toll-road must be one of the last in the country, running along the top of the sandy cliff down into Folkestone through trees with exciting views of the sea.

SANDGATE CASTLE

THE ROYAL MILITARY CANAL
AT SEABROOK

HYTHE AND THE MARSH FROM SUGARLOAF HILL

FOLKESTONE HARBOUR

Between Hythe and Sandgate (a village at about two miles from Hythe) I first saw the *French coast*. The chalk cliffs at Calais are as plain to the view as possible, and also the land, which they tell me is near Boulogne.

Folkestone lies under a Hill here, as Reigate does in Surrey, only here the sea is open to your right as you come along. The corn is very early here, and very fine. *All cut*, even the *beans*; and they will be ready to *cart* in a day or two. Folkestone is now a little place; probably a quarter part as big as it was formerly. Here is a church one hundred and twenty feet long and fifty feet wide. It is a sort of little Cathedral. The church-yard has evidently been three times as large as it is now ...

The belt of chalk that provides such characteristic landscape in northern Hertfordshire, the North Downs of Surrey, Hampshire and even The White Cliffs of Dover, is all the same geological formation. Accompanied by a layer of sandy underscarp it runs from Kent in an approximate 'V' shape, around the watershed of the Thames and up into East Anglia. Outside Folkestone the range of chalk hills stands out, not only with its white-faced escarpments but also with its steep-sided, round-topped contours. Sugarloaf Hill is on the line followed by The Pilgrims' Way and The North Downs Way. From here I could see right back over the coastline from Hythe to Dungeness, and inland over the Marsh to where the land begins to rise. This was where I first saw the coast of France on the journey. From Folkestone The North Downs Way runs along the top of the cliff towards Dover. Shakespeare Cliff, which must be the most famous cliff in the country, has on its top a Borstal, out of bounds to the public.

Hundreds of thousands of people go through Dover every year, but very few actually go to it. Cobbett's description of its layout has never been bettered. Dominated by Western Heights on one side and the Castle Hill on the other, it lies like a seething chasm. There are some surprisingly good views from either side over the Downs, though behind the town there is nothing but industrial development.

Dover
Monday evening, Sept. 1st.

I got here this evening about six o'clock, having come to-day thirty-six miles; but I must defer my remarks on the country between Folkestone and this place; a most interesting spot, and well worthy of particular attention. What place I shall date from *after Dover*, I am by no means *certain*; but, be it from what place it may, the continuation of my Journal shall be published, in due course. If the Atlantic Ocean could not cut off the communication between me and my readers, a mere strip of water, not much wider than an American river, will hardly do it. I am, in real truth, undecided, as yet, whether I shall go on to France, or back to the *Wen*. I think I shall, when I go out of this Inn, toss the bridle upon my horse's neck, and *let him decide for me*. I am sure he is more fit to decide on such a point than our Ministers are to decide on any point connected with the happiness, greatness, and honour of this kingdom.

Wednesday evening, 3rd Sept.
On Monday I was balancing my own mind whether I should go to France or not. To-day I have decided the question in the negative, and shall set off this evening for the Isle of Thanet; that spot so famous for corn.

I broke off without giving an account of the country between Folkestone and Dover, which is a very interesting one in itself, and was peculiarly interesting to me on many accounts.

I have often mentioned, in describing the parts of the country over which I have travelled; I have often mentioned the *chalk-ridge* and also the *sand-ridge*, which I had traced, running parallel with each other from about Farnham, in Surrey, to Sevenoaks, in Kent. The reader must remember how particular I have been to observe that, in going up from Chilworth and Albury, through Dorking, Reigate, Godstone, and so on, the two chains, or ridges, approach so near to each other, that, in many places, you actually have a chalk-bank to your right and a sand-bank to your left, at not more than forty yards from each other … I was always desirous to ascertain whether these chains, or ridges, continued on thus *to the sea*. I have now found that they do. And, if you go out into the channel, at Folkestone, there you see a sand-cliff and a chalk-cliff … The land is like what it is at Reigate, a very steep hill; a hill of full a mile high, and bending exactly in the same manner as the hill at Reigate does. The turnpike-road winds up it and goes over it in exactly the same manner as that at Reigate. The land to the south of the hill begins a poor, thin, white loam upon the chalk soon gets to be a very fine, rich loam upon the chalk; goes on till it mingles the chalky loam with the sandy loam; and thus it goes on down to the sea-beach, or to the edge of the cliff …

From the hill, you keep descending all the way to Dover, a distance of about six miles, and it is absolutely six miles of down hill. On your right, you have the lofty land which forms a series of chalk cliffs, from the top of which you look into the sea; on your left, you have ground that goes rising up from you in the same sort of way. The turnpike-road goes down the middle of a valley, each side of which, as far as you can see, may be about a mile and a half. It is six miles long, you will remember; and here, therefore, with very little interruption, very few chasms, there are *eighteen square miles of corn*. It is a patch such as you very seldom see, and especially of corn so good as it is here. I should think that the wheat all along here would average pretty nearly four quarters to the acre. A few oats are sown. A great deal of barley, and that a very fine crop.

The town of Dover is like other sea-port towns; but really, much more clean, and with less blackguard people in it than I ever observed in any sea-port before. It is a most picturesque place, to be sure. On one side of it rises, upon the top of a very steep hill, the Old Castle, with all its fortifications. On the other side of it there is another chalk-hill, the side of which is pretty nearly perpendicular, and rises up from sixty to an hundred feet higher than the tops of the houses, which stand pretty nearly close to the foot of the hill.

I got into Dover rather late. It was dark when I was going down the street towards the quay. I happened to look up, and was quite astonished to perceive cows grazing upon a spot apparently fifty feet above the tops of the houses, and measuring horizontally not, perhaps, more than ten or twenty feet from a line which would have formed a continuation into the air. I went up to the same spot, the next day, myself; and you actually look down upon the houses, as you look out of a window, upon people in the street. The valley that runs down from Folkestone, is, when it gets to Dover, crossed by another valley that runs down from Canterbury, or, at least, from the Canterbury direction. It is in the gorge of this cross valley that Dover is built. The two chalk-hills jut out into the sea, and the water that comes up between them forms a harbour for this ancient, most interesting, and beautiful place. On the hill to the North, stands the Castle of Dover, which is fortified in the ancient manner, except on the sea-side, where it has the steep *cliff* for a fortification. On the South side of the town, the hill is, I believe, rather more lofty than that on the North side; and here is that cliff which is described by Shakespeare in the Play of King Lear. It is fearfully steep, certainly. Very nearly perpendicular for a considerable distance. The grass grows well, to the very tip of the cliff; and you see cows and sheep grazing there with as much unconcern as if grazing in the bottom of a valley. …

Sandwich
Wednesday night, 3 Sept.

I got to this place about half an hour after the ringing of the eight o'clock bell, or Curfew, which I heard at about two miles distance from the place.

OAK STREET, DEAL

OLD DEAL

I was glad to get out and away, on the A258 road again, to the open landscape where the large rolling fields are typical of chalk country. The old turnpike road to Deal runs through some of the loveliest pasture. Here the grazing cattle, more lively than their usual docile selves, actually appear to be enjoying life. Just past the turning off to St. Margaret's at Cliffe, the road runs through a small wood and here through the trees is an expansive view of the countryside to the north; cows graze pasture, unencumbered by pylons, on the far side of a small valley. The nearside had just been ploughed. At Ringwould I took the B2057 back towards the sea to come into Deal along the beach. The village of Kingsdown has a very interesting little street leading down to the sea, though the road along the beach is lined with neo-Georgian houses, facing out to sea. Walmer Castle stands here, dignified in its modern surroundings. Deal is busy, with interesting narrow streets around the sea front. Sadly, however, it has not escaped the inevitable coffee bars and amusement arcades. There is a cafe on the front called 'Chez Maureen', (in Kingsdown there is another called 'Chez Maurice', perhaps the two should get together). The back streets along the sea front to the north of the town evoke the old Deal in the heyday of sail, when 'the Downs' offshore were the busiest sheltered anchorage in the world. The Goodwin Sands have claimed more wrecks than any other sandbank in the world and 'the Downs' provided the perfect shelter. Right at the north end of the town is the coastguard station and Sandown Castle, though only a few stones remain of the latter. From here, the scene away over the shingle bank towards Ramsgate and inland over the flats towards Sandwich is exceptional. From this point I could also see the looming mass of Richborough Power Station dominating so much of the area around it.

From the town of Dover you come up the Castle-Hill, and have a most beautiful view from the top of it. You have the sea, the chalk cliffs of Calais, the high land at Boulogne, the town of Dover just under you, the valley towards Folkestone, and the much more beautiful valley towards Canterbury; and, going on a little further, you have the Downs and the Essex or Suffolk coast in full view, with a most beautiful corn country to ride along through. The corn was chiefly cut between Dover and Walmer. The barley almost all cut and tied up in sheaf. Nothing but the beans seemed to remain standing alone here. They are not quite so good as the rest of the corn; but they are by no means bad. When I came to the village of Walmer, I enquired for the Castle; that famous place, where Pitt, Dundas, Perceval and all the whole tribe of plotters against the French Revolution had carried on their plots. After coming through the village of Walmer, you see the entrance of the Castle away to the right. It is situated pretty nearly on the water's edge, and at the bottom of a little dell, about a furlong or so from the turnpike-road …

Deal is a most villanous place. It is full of filthy-looking people. Great desolation of abomination has been going on here; tremendous barracks, partly pulled down and partly tumbling down, and partly occupied by soldiers. Every thing seems upon the perish. I was glad to hurry along through it, and to leave its inns and public-houses to be occupied by the tarred, and trowsered, and blue-

and-buff crew whose very vicinage I always detest. From Deal you come along to Upper Deal, which it seems was the original village; thence upon a beautiful road to Sandwich, which is a rotten Borough. Rottenness, putridity is excellent for land, but bad for Boroughs. This place, which is as villanous a hole as one would wish to see, is surrounded by some of the finest land in the world. Along on one side of it, lies a marsh. On the other sides of it is land which they tell me bears *seven quarters* of wheat to an acre. It is certainly very fine; for I saw large pieces of radish-seed on the road side; this seed is grown for the seedsmen in London; and it will grow on none but rich land. All the corn is carried here except some beans and some barley.

TO DEAL

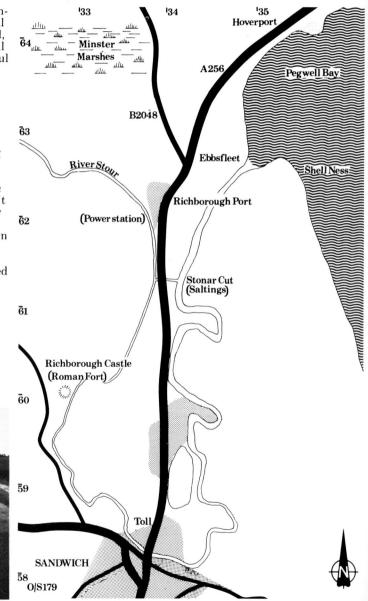

The road to Sandwich, a continuation of the old turnpike road, is very low and marshy. Sandwich today is separated from the sea by the Royal St. George's Golf Links, whose fame now overshadows the history of the ancient Cinque Port. The sleepy town is a maze of little alleys and beautiful old buildings with a Dutch and Flemish influence. A great many of the less important houses are sadly in very bad repair. Just outside the town on the A257 to Canterbury is the small turning to Richborough Castle. This is the first Roman fort built in the country by the Emperor Claudius at the time of his invasion in AD 43 and remaining the port of entry into the country during most of the Roman occupation. The road that leads up to the site is a mess, with scrap-metal yards, deserted cars lying around, polluted streams and the remains of the railway which has fallen into ruin.

Sandwich is on the southerly tip of a huge loop of the river Stour. As the sea retreated, it left some very fertile soil on the drained marshes. It is now the site of Richborough Port and a vast chemical works that has almost swallowed up the whole marsh. The small remaining part is a maze of drains and sewers. To get onto the Thanet Road from Sandwich, it is necessary to pass under the Barbican Toll Bridge, and over the river. The saltings that Cobbett mentions have only recently disappeared. They used to be near what is now the 'Red Lion' pub, on the road, by the Stonar Cut. Richborough Power Station cannot possibly be missed; it stands over the marshes, sending out its pylon feelers all over the countryside. Strangely it commands respect.

ST. PETER'S, SANDWICH

Canterbury
Thursday afternoon, 4th Sept.

In quitting Sandwich, you immediately cross a river up which vessels bring coals from the sea. This marsh is about a couple of miles wide. It begins at the sea-beach, opposite the Downs, to my right hand, coming from Sandwich, and it wheels round to my left and ends at the sea-beach, opposite Margate roads. This marsh was formerly covered with the sea, very likely; and hence the land within this sort of semicircle, the name of which is Thanet, was called an *Isle*. It is, in fact, an island now, for the same reason that Portsea is an island, and that New York is an island; for there certainly is the water in this river that goes round and connects one part of the sea with the other. I had to cross this river, and to cross the marsh, before I got into the famous Isle of Thanet, which it was my intention to cross. Soon after crossing the river, I passed by a place for making salt …

THE BARBICAN, SANDWICH

BEHIND QUAY STREET

STONAR MARSHES

Just before the road rises up onto the chalk of the Isle of Thanet, it skirts Pegwell Bay. Here at low tide the sand flats are exposed over a distance of two miles and there are usually lugworm diggers dotted all over the sands. Here also in the little pools nearer to the shore are the finest samphire plants that I have ever seen. Known as marsh samphire or glasswort it thrives on salt-marshes and some sandy shores. It is said that the plant is ready for picking on the longest day, June 21st, and the best plants are those that have been 'washed by every tide'. Young samphire makes a fresh and tangy salad, although somewhat salty, but the older plant can be boiled for about ten minutes and served with butter. It can even be pickled. Here is better samphire even than that found in East Anglia.

Pegwell Bay was also the landing place of the Saxons in 449. On the cliffs just by the hoverport there is a replica of a Viking ship, the Hugin, that was actually rowed across the North Sea from Denmark in 1948.

RICHBOROUGH LEVEL CROSSING

Salt Marsh

This is a desolate place, neither inland nor shore.
In the shelter of the creek, gulls confabulate.
We have come past the huts where the pungent smell
of dead fish lives. We have come past the quay,
and the shingle with its upturned boats and heaps
of discarded barnacled mussel and whelk shells
to a close-tufted marsh carpet of seablite and purslane
that hugs the mud under a hurrying wind
undulating over uneven contours,
rolled out and flattened by the low, cold sky.

I have stumbled into a grey parenthesis
suspended somewhere between growing and drowning.
In the distance is the sea, strange
and dangerous.   The children call.
                              They have finished
exploring, and want to go home.

Shona Burns

LUGWORM DIGGERS, PEGWELL BAY

PEGWELL BAY, SAMPHIRE IN FOREGROUND

Can any man tell why we should still be paying five, or six, or seven shillings a bushel for salt, instead of one? We did pay fifteen shillings a bushel, tax. And why is two shillings a bushel kept on? Because, if they were taken off, the salt-tax-gathering crew must be discharged! This tax of two shillings a bushel, causes the consumer to pay five, at the least, more than he would if there were no tax at all! When, great God! when shall we be allowed to enjoy God's gifts, in freedom, as the people of France enjoy them? On the marsh I found the same sort of sheep as on Romney Marsh; but the cattle here are chiefly Welsh; black, and called runts. They are nice hardy cattle; and, I am told, that this is the description of cattle that they fat all the way up on this north side of Kent. When I got upon the corn land in the Isle of Thanet, I got into a garden indeed. There is hardly any fallow; comparatively few turnips. It is a country of corn. Most of the harvest is in; but there are some fields of wheat and of barley not yet housed. A great many pieces of lucerne, and all of them very fine. I left Ramsgate to my right about three miles, and went right across the island to Margate; but that place is so thickly settled with stock-jobbing cuckolds, at this time of the year, that, having no fancy to get their horns stuck into me, I turned away to my left when I got within about half a mile of the town. I got to a little hamlet, where I breakfasted; but could get no corn for my horse, and no bacon for me!

The whole coastline of the North Foreland is one great housing estate. The road that Cobbett must have taken was as rural as could be imagined. It is still open, but the road has been enlarged and the tops of the buildings can be seen peering over the hills. This is the overspill from Ramsgate and Broadstairs. The battalions of houses march steadfastly onwards, though the fields away from the suburbs are extremely beautiful. There are not many trees on this part of the chalk and the tops of the hills are very exposed.

Monkton lies to the east of Minster. Here the village street lies below the main road, the A253, which runs along the crest of the hill towards Sarre. At Monkton I saw the first oast house since I began this journey at Tenterden in the Weald.

MARGATE, THE FRONT

VIEW OF BROADSTAIRS FROM NEAR ST. PETER'S

THE STOUR VALLEY

THE RIVER WANTSUM

OLD WINDMILL, SARRE

The A253 between Monkton and Sarre is open and wind-swept. To the south the land falls away to the Stour Marshes or what used to be the sea-bed of the channel around the Isle of Thanet. Below Gore Street is a bridge over the Stour, at the point it becomes a single channel joined by the Great Stour from Canterbury and the Little Stour that flows from above Wickhambreaux.

As Cobbett mentions, the River Wantsum flows under the road, at the other side of Sarre. This is the westerly boundary of Thanet. The road then follows the Roman road along the valley of the Great Stour into Canterbury. Here the land becomes much more cultivated. There are acres of orchards on the south side of the valley towards Wickhambreaux and Littlebourne. On the A28 into Canterbury Sturry, (Cobbett calls the village Steady) is almost part of suburban Canterbury. Nothing remains of the barracks of which Cobbett complains; just the odd pub with a military connection, such as 'The Volunteer'. The area is now a residential and light industrial outpost of the town.

All was corn around me. Barns, I should think, two hundred feet long; ricks of enormous size and most numerous; crops of wheat, five quarters to an acre, on the average; and a public-house without either bacon or corn! The labourers' houses, all along through this island, beggarly in the extreme. The people dirty, poor-looking; ragged, but particularly *dirty*. The men and boys with dirty faces, and dirty smock-frocks, and dirty shirts; and, good God! what a difference between the wife of a labouring man here, and the wife of a labouring man in the forests and woodlands of Hampshire and Sussex! Invariably have I observed, that the richer the soil, and the more destitute of woods; that is to say, the more purely a corn country, the more miserable the labourers. The cause is this, the great, the big bull frog grasps all. In this beautiful island every inch of land is appropriated by the rich. No hedges, no ditches, no commons, no grassy lanes: a country divided into great farms; a few trees surround the great farmhouse. All the rest is bare of trees; and the wretched labourer has not a stick of wood, and has no place for a pig or cow to graze, or even to lie down upon. The rabbit countries are the countries for labouring men. There the ground is not so valuable. There it is not so easily appropriated by the few. Here, in this island, the work is almost all done by the horses. The horses plough the ground; they sow the ground; they hoe the ground; they carry the corn home; they thresh it out; and they carry it to market: nay, in this island,

they *rake* the ground; they rake up the straggling straws and ears; so that they do the whole, except the reaping and the mowing. It is impossible to have an idea of any thing more miserable than the state of the labourers in this part of the country.

After coming by Margate, I passed a village called Monckton, and another called Sarr. At Sarr there is a bridge, over which you come out of the island, as you go into it over the bridge at Sandwich. At Monckton they had *seventeen men work-*

ing on the roads, though the harvest was not quite in, and though, of course, it had all to be threshed out; but, at Monckton, they had *four threshing machines;* and they have three threshing machines at Sarr, though there, also, they have several men upon the roads! ...

At Sarr, or a little way further back, I saw a man who had just begun to reap a field of canary seed. The plants were too far advanced to be cut in order to be bleached for the making of plat; but I got the reaper to select me a few green

stalks that grew near a bush that stood on the outside of the piece. These I have brought on with me, in order to give them a trial! At Sarr I began to cross the marsh, and had, after this, to come through the village of Up-Street, and another village called Steady, before I got to Canterbury. At Up-Street I was struck with the words written upon a board which was fastened upon a pole, which pole was standing in a garden near a neat little box of a house. The words were these. 'Paradise Place. *Spring guns and steel traps are set here.*' A pretty idea it must give us of Paradise to know that spring guns and steel traps are set in it! This is doubtless some stock-jobber's place; for, in the first place, the name is likely to have been selected by one of that crew; and, in the next place, whenever any of them go to the country, they look upon it that they are to be in a sort of warfare against every thing around them. They invariably look upon every labourer as a thief.

As you approach Canterbury, from the Isle of Thanet, you have another instance of the squanderings of the lawyer Ministers ...

They have lately had races at Canterbury; and the Mayor and Aldermen, in order to get the Prince Leopold to attend them, presented him with the Freedom of the City; but it rained all the time and he did not come! The Mayor and Aldermen do not understand things half so well as this German Gentleman, who has managed his matters as well, I think, as any one that I ever heard of.

THE KINGS SCHOOL SHOP,
CANTERBURY

KENT ORCHARDS

DUNKIRK

Canterbury is still a most attractive city. The Cathedral must be one of the greatest shrines. Christchurch Gate is in a perilous condition due to the vibration caused by the continual clicking of camera shutters. The boy who was given sixpence for holding Cobbett's horse would have had no idea of the machines that would replace him in the future—the parking meter is a common feature of Canterbury, spoiling the atmosphere for the sake of modern-day efficiency.

The A2 from Canterbury, travelling west, has become a dual carriageway and it is very difficult to find the old road, except by weaving in and out, or rather on and off, the new road. Boughton Hill is just beyond the village of Dunkirk and still affords one of the most breath-taking views. On a clear day it is possible to see Faversham and right over the Swale to the Isle of Sheppey. Unfortunately the middle distance is now developed and distracting to the eye. The A2 continues into Faversham, a town surrounded by hop groves and apple farms in the true Kent spirit, and still holding onto the seafaring traditions that were its main business.

NEAR BOUGHTON STREET

This fine old town, or, rather, city, is remarkable for cleanliness and niceness, notwithstanding it has a Cathedral in it. The country round it is very rich, and this year, while the hops are so bad in most other parts, they are not so very bad, just about Canterbury.

Elverton Farm near Faversham
Friday morning, Sept. 6

In going through Canterbury, yesterday, I gave a boy sixpence to hold my horse, while I went into the Cathedral, just to thank St Swithin for the trick that he had played my friends, the Quakers. Led along by the wet weather till after the harvest had actually begun, and then to find the weather turn fine, all of a sudden! This must have soused them pretty decently ... The land where I am now is equal to that of the Isle of Thanet. The harvest is nearly over, and all the crops have been prodigiously fine. In coming from Canterbury, you come to the top of a hill, called Baughton Hill, at four miles from Canterbury on the London road; and you there look down into one of the finest flats in England. A piece of marsh comes up nearly to Faversham; and, at the edge of that marsh lies the farm where I now am. The land here is a deep loam upon chalk; and this is also the nature of the land in The Isle of Thanet and all the way from that to Dover. The orchards grow well upon this soil. The trees grow finely, the fruit is large and of fine flavour.

Faversham Creek runs behind Abbey Street and little paths with such names as 'Smack Alley' run from the mariners' cottages down to the water. Here there once stood shipyards, sail lofts, maltings and wharves. Today the waterfront is strangely vacant except for the occasional vessel making a visit.

Where argosies have wooed the breeze,
The simple sheep are feeding now;
And near and far across the bar
The ploughman whistles at the plough;
Where once the long waves washed the shore,

Larks from their lowly lodgings soar.
Below the down the stranded town
Nears far away the rollers beat;
About the wall the seabirds call;
The salt wind murmurs through the street;
Forlorn the sea's forsaken bride
Awaits the end that shall betide.

John Davidson (1857-1909)

In 1821 I gave Mr Wm. Waller, who lives here, some American apple-cuttings; and he has now some as fine New-town Pippins as one would wish to see. They are very large of their sort; very free in their growth; and they promise to be very fine apples of the kind …

My American apples, when I left Kensington, promised to be very fine; and the apples, which I have frequently mentioned as being upon cuttings imported last Spring, promised to come to perfection; a thing which, I believe, we have not an instance of before.

LEFT. THE 'EYE OF THE WIND'
IN FAVERSHAM CREEK,
SEPTEMBER 1976

FAVERSHAM CREEK C. 1900 (Reproduced by kind permission of the Faversham Society).

The Huntingdon Journal

through the counties of
Middlesex, Essex, Hertfordshire and Cambridgeshire.

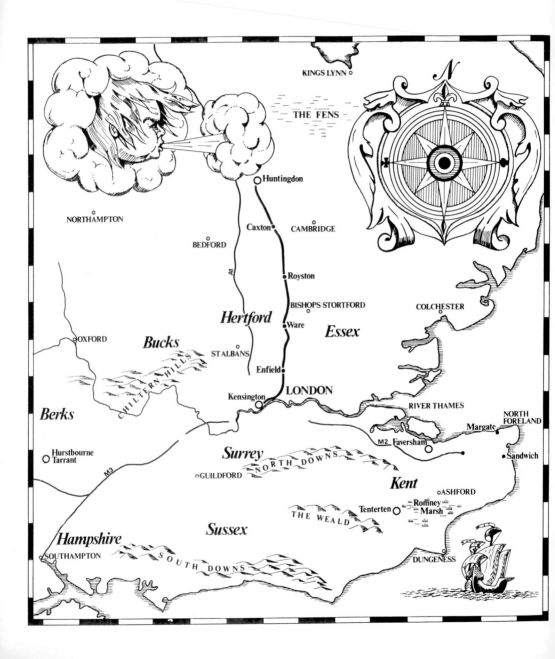

Leaving the city of London, bound North, I followed the old Roman Ermine Street, which was the first main road in the country, now called the A10. I drove due north through the market streets of Stoke Newington, the village home of Daniel Defoe for nearly twenty years from 1674, and then on to the Victorian sprawl of Tottenham and Edmonton. Across the Lea Valley to the east lies Walthamstow, an area that William Morris described in his childhood as :—

'all flat pasture, except for a few gardens ... the wide green sea of the Essex marshland, with the great domed line of the sky and the sun shining down in one flood of peaceful light over the long distance.'

Today that peaceful open landscape is broken and obscured by clumps of residential development, engineering works, waste ground and reservoirs. Nothing remains of William Morris' youthful view. The Lea Valley runs due north but this stretch of outer London is solidly built up.

From Edmonton the aspect grows grimmer. The houses stand identical and drab for square miles on end, a planner's dream. It is a relief to turn west off the A10 to Enfield. With a diminishing population Enfield is the last stronghold of suburbia before the open country; but somehow it has retained its own character as a town.

It centres around Church Street and 'The Town'. The parish church is set amongst trees with weather-boarded houses nearby. Holly Walk is a leafy path running towards the New River and Gentleman's Row. The New River was constructed in the years 1603-1613 to provide fresh water for London. It ran from Amwell springs near Ware to Islington and its architect, Sir Hugh Myddleton, lived in Enfield. The river runs through a green meadow area called Chase Side. The beauty of the area is complemented by the gentility of Gentleman's Row, a collection of finely preserved eighteenth century houses, still the finest street in Enfield and now shut off from the traffic.

Charles Lamb stayed at No 17, Clarendon Cottage, in 1827. The houses have fine gardens and amongst such peace and grandeur it is difficult to appreciate that the busy commercial High Street is a few hundred yards away. To the north the river frontage is modern but attractive, a terrace of a hundred yards or so before the river winds away over playing fields beyond Horseshoe Lane. The old road north from Enfield, the A105, starts as Silver Street where there are still some fine Georgian houses and a lovely white weather-boarded house that belonged to Joseph Whittaker, the almanac man. Continuing past the new Civic Centre the road turns into Baker Street and gradually rises up to Forty Hill.

ST. MICHAEL'S CHURCH
THE NEW RIVER AT HORSESHOE LANE
THE NEW RIVER

GENTLEMAN'S ROW

The road becomes a rural lane, narrow and twisting, lined with overhanging trees and the old village houses set back in their own grounds. The gates to Forty Hall are on the top of the hill. This is a lovely Jacobean house set in open grounds, now used as an archeological and historical museum. It was built in the 1630's by Sir Nicholas Raynton, a Lord Mayor of London, and the gardens and park are said to have been laid out by the great French gardener Le Notre. There is a lake in front of the house and a beautiful avenue of lime trees stretch away down a gentle hill to a stream. Here there is good walking in open rough parkland with the wooded horizon of Epping Forest to the east. The lane, now called Bull's Cross, runs on down over Maiden Bridge, one of the places where Sir Walter Raleigh is supposed to have muddied his cloak for his queen. Myddleton House is opposite Turkey Street that runs east from the A105 to join the A10. This is the headquarters of the Lea Valley Regional Park Authority. It is hoped to turn the whole of the Lea Valley eventually into a vast recreational area stretching from Bromley by Bow, in dockland, north to Ware. As a result of a plan prepared by the Civic Trust in 1964 there are currently 2000 acres of land, much reclaimed from the derelict areas and gravel workings known as 'the backyard of London'.

An annual expenditure of three million pounds has provided a marina, riding centre, cycle circuit, and leisure stadium. This re-established countryside can be discovered too with nature trails and access to twenty three miles of the river Lea. The Authority has recently bought a farm to the north of Enfield to be opened to the public, so that all can see and appreciate its working.

FORTY HALL

Back on Bull's Cross, the A105, I came to the 'Pied Bull' pub, which in the days when the area was the Royal Chase, was a dog kennel. Today the road turns sharply to the east to join the A10 but I carried on into Bull's Cross Ride and then on through Theobalds Park. Here, incongruous and forgotten, right away in the heart of the woods, looms the old Temple Bar, built by Sir Christopher Wren in 1672 as a gateway to the City of London. Once prominently strad-dling the Strand and Fleet Street, now in its rural seclusion it is difficult to find.

Ignore the signs to 'private estate' and follow the 'Public Footpath' notice. Still in the car I followed the track into the wood, passing Theobalds College and some stables to the right. There seemed to be some development going on though tucked away, but after a right turn deeper into the forest, I eventually came to the monument. It was a thundery afternoon in summer with clouds accumulating. Just visible through the trees, utterly out of place in a clearing, stood this vast seventeenth century archway with ivy growing up the sides, surrounded by a military barbed wire fence. In 1888 Sir Henry Bruce Meux transferred it from Fleet Street to his park, Theobalds, where it has since stood, neglected and decaying. Sadly it would need at least three quarters of a million pounds to make it even safe.

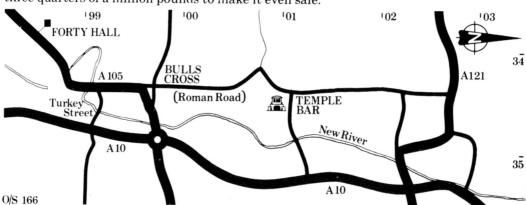

TEMPLE BAR

Moving back towards the A10, I kept on catching glimpses through the trees of beautiful rolling countryside. Highlighted by the sun the farmland looked reassuring. It was strange to think that no more than a mile down the road was the great scar of the A10.

I planned to visit Waltham Abbey and even to venture up to High Beach in Epping Forest on the other side of the valley. Suburbia loomed again. I crossed the main road and followed Bull's Cross Lane up over New River to Waltham Cross. This area must be the worst example of ribbon development. Anyone travelling north has to cross this wasteland of brick and glass, multi-storey car parks and dirty yards, right in the middle of which is the Waltham Cross. In fact to approach Waltham Abbey you have to go round the Cross. The Cross itself was part of the High Street, before Waltham Cross was smitten with the one-way disease. It is in fact one of the Eleanor Crosses that were erected by Edward I to commemorate the resting places of his dead queen, Eleanor of Castile, on the way from Harby in Leicestershire where she died, to Westminster Abbey.

WALTHAM CROSS

Heading up the A121 East towards Waltham Abbey the road finally opens out to the Lea Valley running north to south. Yet another one-way system here protects a charming town. The main road veers off to the north-east while the narrow High Street welcomes the curious traveller. The great white tower of the abbey church, visible for miles around, dominates the little market town. Waltham Abbey was once the richest church in Essex being so near to the royal hunting forest and thus patronised by the nobility. Here King Harold stopped to pray on his way to the battle of Hastings and it was here also that his body is supposed to have been returned. A stone marks the spot where his grave is meant to be. The church itself is magnificent; Pevsner compares it in stature to Durham Cathedral. It stands in the grounds of the Abbey, now beautifully looked after as part of the Lea Valley Regional Park. There is a moat full of bullrushes. The Cornmill Stream, famous for its swans, runs through the gardens and the old gate of the Abbey before disappearing under the road in front of the church. Here there is a very special atmosphere, perhaps because the church is so impressive and its history so vivid. Looking out as it used to once over the stark Essex marshes, it is easy to imagine the sound of approaching armies and the clash of their steel. Not far from the Abbey is the river whose banks

THE ABBEY GATE

THE APPROACH TO WALTHAM ABBEY

THE ABBEY CHURCH & THE CORNMILL STREAM

THE RIVER LEA

to the north are usually dotted with fishermen. The skyline is refreshingly open except for the pylons that disappear into the distance. The little town crouches under the shadow of the church. There is a small market twice a week in the ancient market square, Romeland, and the narrow Sun Street contain some fine buildings which reflect the tranquility of this little place only a few miles from the heaving metropolis. As a small detour, I went up to High Beach, one of the most popular spots in Epping Forest. From here some 109 metres above sea-level the view over the valley is superb. Beyond Waltham Abbey town, the A112 runs south to Chingford and about a mile along on the left is the road, clearly marked High Beach. As you climb up into the forest the trees become thicker but all of a sudden you come out into the clearing to look right out over the valley. The Abbey is clearly visible and shines white in the sun. The sound of the bells from the valley below inspired Tennyson, who lived here in the 1830's, to write 'In Memoriam'.

HIGH BEACH

Epping Forest is London's forest and a wonderful place to escape to; even at weekends it is possible to push deeper into the forest to escape the cars.

132

ENFIELD LOCK

Back again in Hertfordshire and on the route I passed through a suburb called 'Freezywater', the chillness of its name was apt on the day I travelled through it. Just south of Waltham Cross, on the river, is Enfield Lock. This is the home of the Small Arms Factory, that which most people associate with the name Enfield. The powder from the one-time mills at Waltham Abbey was brought by the river to the factory. 'The Ordinance' pub still stands nearby and it may be that the walnut trees along the riverside below the lock were used to supply wood for the gunstocks. Now the river gently winds away below the lock; again an ideal place for fishermen and a nostalgic walk along the tow-path. The great barges carrying iron and coal have all been replaced with pleasure boats, putting up and down the river.

LEA VALLEY LANDSCAPE

RIVER LEA BELOW ENFIELD LOCK

Before entering Ware, the road passes through two small
towns, Broxbourne and Hoddesdon. A dual carriageway now
bypasses both but endeavouring to keep away from that, I
turned off onto the B176 through the north of Cheshunt.
Broxbourne is no more than a series of coaching houses and
hamlets around which development has spread. Set well
away from Ermine Street towards the river is St Augustine's Church, which is approached through a wonderful
avenue of lime trees. The church is set in a common that
separated the road from the meadows of the river. This has
become one of the largest complexes belonging to the Lea
Valley Regional Park. There is currently under construc-
tion a marina and there are spaces for camping and walking.
Though hardly rural it is a pleasant recreational area and
the authorities should be congratulated for realising their
ambitions. The old Broxbourne Mill, which was burnt down
in 1949, is being partially restored. The only disadvantages
are the inevitable mobile snack wagon and the mess that
invariably ensues. Footpaths are very well signposted to
Dobb's Weir, another park area to the North, and there are
plans for nature trails and extensive clearance of waste
areas. It is sad to see a house with a garden to the river
displaying a huge sign prohibiting fishing on the *opposite*
side of the river.

ST. AUGUSTINE'S CHURCH

APPROACH TO THE CHURCH

Royston,
Monday morning, 21st Jan. 1822
Came from London, yesterday
noon, to this town on my way
to Huntingdon. My road was
through Ware. Royston is just
within the line (on the Cambridgeshire side), which divides
Hertfordshire from Cambridgeshire. On this road, as on almost
all the others going from it, the
enormous *Wen* has swelled out
to the distance of about six or
seven miles.—The land till you
come nearly to Ware which is in
Hertfordshire, and which is
twenty-three miles from the
Wen, is chiefly a strong and
deep loam, with the gravel a
good distance from the surface.
The land is good wheat-land;
but I observed only three fields
of swedish turnips in the 23
miles, and no wheat drilled. The
wheat is sown on ridges of great
width here and there; sometimes on ridges of ten, at others
on ridges of seven, on those of
five, four, three and even two,
feet wide. Yet the bottom is
manifestly not very wet generally; and that there is not a
bottom of clay is clear from the
poor growth of the oak trees.

RIVER LEA, BROXBOURNE

Hoddesdon is a larger town to the north though running directly on from Broxbourne's sprawl. Noted for its inns in the coaching days, it is now more of a healthy shopping centre. Out towards the river again is a small area used as a bird sanctuary, run by the Royal Society for the Protection of Birds, and the remains of Rye House stand to the side. This is the place where in 1683 an assassination of Charles II was plotted, unsuccessfully. Only the gatehouse remains which until recently was also crumbling. It has now been restored by the Lea Valley Regional Park Authority and, although not yet completely open to the public, it is planned to use it as a museum and exhibition centre. It is rather overshadowed by the modern power station nearby.

WARE IN THE 1890'S (Author's collection)

The Ermine Street runs up Great Amwell Hill and down into Ware. Although I am told it is approached best from Hertford, Ware sits prettily in the Lea Valley with meadows stretching around it. From a distance the skyline is jagged with an abundance of old maltings, most of which are now redundant. The town is a place of great contrasts; there are streets with houses so dilapidated that they look positively dangerous. There are some very prosperous houses in a town that was once the centre of middle-class fashion. The High Street winds from the river bridge round to St Mary's Church, where it becomes Baldock Street. On the south side of the street there are, disguised as shops, some of the most beautiful houses with long deep gardens stretching down to the river. At the end of the gardens are gazebos, little weather-boarded or tiled summer houses, built out over the water. These are clearly visible from the opposite side of the river where there has been extensive work to the banks, involving deep piling and concreting. This may well be very necessary work, but hardly complementary to the river that Sir Isaak Walton immortalised in his 'Compleat Angler'. The view does give you some idea of the civility that once was; the faded backs of the eighteenth century houses and the long overgrown gardens, the crumbling maltings backing onto the river and the gazebos, their vacant windows

GAZEBOS, WARE

OLD WARE

staring blankly across the water. All that is a better sight than the faceless housing development behind.

I walked over a footbridge, onto the north bank and found myself back in the High Street again, by the church. Walking along by the shops, I noticed the tall coaching gateways alongside the houses. These opened out in many cases to beautiful yards and fascinating alleys. I found myself in one, rather smaller than the others, by a carpet shop, and there was an overgrown wall with a small door. I had to go through. It led into the most attractive secret garden. The sun was high, and a barely discernible garden path through brambles and cow parsley led me deeper into this English jungle a foot at a time. There were cherries, plums and apples hanging in my way. My guide, an overgrown privet hedge, stopped abruptly at a clearing with swaying grasses a foot high. I looked up to see the front of one of the gazebos. The glass was broken in the windows and the door was hanging by one hinge. The huge dome of a malting in the next garden dominated the timeless scene. I emerged from this forgotten garden to face once again the bustle of the High Street.

THE FORGOTTEN GARDEN

142

THOMAS CLARKSON MEMORIAL

I left Ware to travel north again on the A10 climbing steeply. At last I reached real country. After all the intimations of it through the Lea Valley, this was the real thing. The road rises and falls as you come to Wadesmill. From the top of the hill you can see the Roman road stretching straight down into the steep valley and up again and away towards High Cross. In the valley runs the river Rib which meets the Lea just east of Ware and which the road crosses by an iron bridge built in 1825. From the other side of the valley the village seems to merge with the river and the new tower of Thundridge church becomes the landmark. Along the valley, a half mile to the east of the road, Wadesmill's old church tower stands covered in creepers and hidden by trees. Dating back to Norman times, it has become the victim of a village which has moved on with the trade to the new road. Halfway up the hill there is a small obelisk that was erected to the memory of Thomas Clarkson in 1879 ... 'who resolved on this spot in 1785 to devote his life to the abolition of the slave trade.'. But far more to the point, from the top of the bank, there is a marvellous view of fields stretching to the horizon. When I was there they had just been harvested and the lines of stubble converging in the distance emphasised the natural

All the trees are shabby in this country; and the eye is incessantly offended by the sight of *pollards,* which are seldom suffered to disgrace even the meanest lands in Hampshire or Sussex. As you approach Ware the bottom becomes chalk of a dirtyish colour, and, in some parts, far below the surface. After you quit Ware, which is a mere market town, the land grows by degrees poorer; the chalk lies nearer and nearer to the surface, till you come to the open common-fields within a few miles of Royston. Along here the land is poor enough. It is not the stiff red loam mixed with large blue-grey flints, lying upon the chalk, such as you see in the north of Hampshire; but a whitish sort of clay, with little yellow flattish stones amongst it; sure signs of a hungry soil. Yet this land bears wheat sometimes.

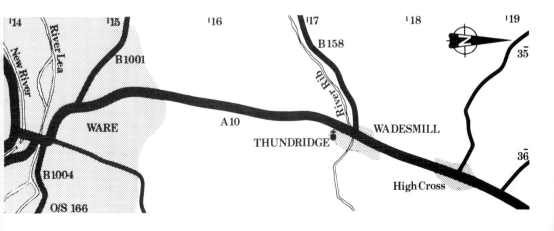

perspective. From the other side of the road, through a small gateway, I found the view I was hoping for back over towards Thundridge.

The Roman road runs north through High Cross and Collier's End, both very well situated villages with interesting old houses on each side of the main highway. It is a cruel irony that the best houses in a village are often those along the main street which, in being part of the trunk road, suffer the greatest assault from streams of traffic and thundering juggernauts.

From the road the fields fold away like vast mazes. The harvest was very early during 1976 because of the extreme summer conditions and the fields had been cut in various directions; pylon-free they sweep to the horizon, an expanse of shifting light and shade. The road through and around Puckeridge is undergoing a great deal of rebuilding and the dual carriageway is being extended to bypass the market town to the west. There is evidence of a Roman settlement on the north side of the town inside the angle of the road, as it turns to the north-west. After Puckeridge the road straddles a small ridge running towards Buntingford. Quite by chance I came across what many consider to be the finest village in Hertfordshire. I turned left off the A10 to Westmill. Although rather 'deliciously English' it really is a beautiful village in a perfect setting, below the ridge with the river Rib running close by through its own meadows. I take the liberty of quoting Humphrey Pakington, the village anthologist, who said, whilst describing the

LOOKING BACK TO THUNDRIDGE

WESTMILL

village at some length; 'The buildings are set mainly round a small informal green where two roads meet. The green slopes down to the eastward ... along the road (to the church) runs a line of stumpy lime trees, while a great chestnut tree raises its burly head above the cottage roofs, rivalling in interest the grey church tower with its leaded spire '. The village green has in fact got a well in the centre; the well housing is modern and carved around the inside edge is: 'Traverse the desert and then you can tell, what treasure exists in the cool deep well '. The houses each have individual plaques with a name in memory of those who lived there. Judging by the names they all seem to be interrelated.

WYDDIAL

Buntingford is another pleasant town sitting squarely either side of the Roman road with the modern development discreetly tucked away behind the coaching façade of the High Street. Towards the north of the town I turned off the road to Wyddial. I passed through an estate of houses built in a series of crescents, each with a character of its own. However, it was like stepping out of their back door when I went over a small bridge and into the shade of a belt of trees. I was really looking for the wide open spaces that are so well known in the regions to the north of the county, where the Chiltern hills open out to the broad harvest fields and on to the chalk plains of the Royston downs. Passing through the village of Wyddial, which itself was blighted by a line of mean-windowed council establishments on one side of the street, I found my view. Wyddial Hall stood on my left; not a very imposing exterior and set well back, its own belt of trees gave way to the broad open space to the north.

It was a hot windless day and against the horizon the combine harvesters were busy gathering the early harvest. The air was full of the distant hum of machines and the lane stretched enticingly away in front of me. It was all here; the grassy verges opening out to wide unbroken fields, the bold trees lining the roads or standing together in copses, the busy silence of open space. This is what E. M. Forster described in his novel 'Howards End', referring to the Hertfordshire countryside as 'England meditative'. If Cobbett had not been in such a hurry to get to Huntingdon he would have appreciated more the beauty of the wide open spaces of eastern Hertfordshire (as impressed as he was by the western parts, particularly Tring). Here, on the threshold of the Wen, no more than 40 miles from the City of London is the real English countryside; no longer intruded upon by tall factory chimneys and mining deposits, or even imprisoned by pylons, the horizon joins the sky in a rare state of freedom.

'ENGLAND MEDITATIVE'

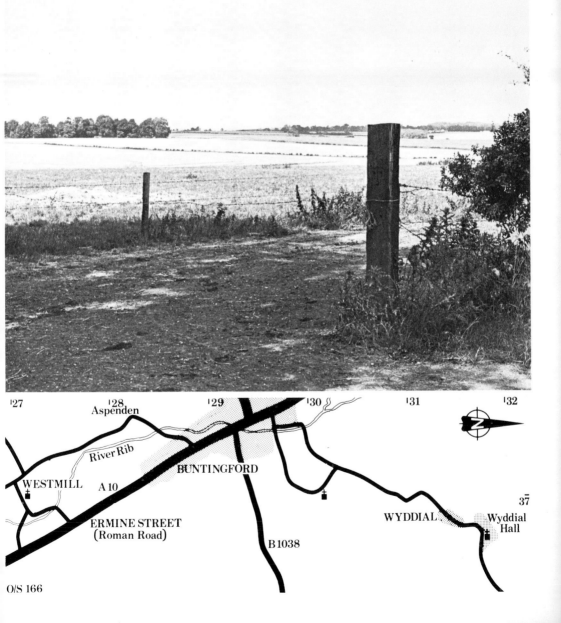

O/S 166

Back on the A1, it was not long after going through Buckland that the road dipped down the hill towards Royston. The view here was magnificent. I turned off to the right down a little road marked Reed. This ran along a great chalk ridge, on either side of which were crops as far as the eye could see. The main landmark on the ridge happened to be the radio mast. I climbed a haystack, adding 10 feet to my calculated 520 feet above sea-level. From here the land sloped down towards Royston and beyond to the watershed of the River Cam and the Fens. In the foreground were a few trees running down the line of a ditch, curiously isolated amongst the acres of stubble stretching away in parallel shades of brown. In the very distance a circular copse of trees stood out like a wart, and the middle distance was complicated by lines of hedges.

DOWN TO WHITELEY HILL

The village of Reed is scattered around the winding lanes and is as windswept as the crest of the hill from which it retreats. There is evidence of there having been an ancient settlement; some villagers believe that it was a colony for retired Roman soldiers and that the 'moats' marked on the map suggest the boundaries of their allotments, but nothing has been proved. The church stands alone in the fields and the remains of what could have been a fortification stands on Periwinkle Hill, suggesting that the ridge, in more hostile days, had been jealously guarded.

THE RIDGE ROAD

Carrying on past the radio mast, the road turns sharply left at a junction and runs straight down the hill until it climbs again, this time to Whiteley Hill, on the other side of the great valley. The view, looking back, is not nearly as impressive but the ridge is clearly visible. The road very soon joins the B1039 and this takes you into Royston through the back of the town. The town of Royston has grown up around the intersection of the Roman Ermine Street, the A10, and the much older Icknield Way. King James I stopped here on his way from Scotland to London after the death of Queen Elizabeth and he returned often to hunt on the 400 acres of heath, most of which exists today as common land. What is left of the old royal hunting lodge still stands in Kneesworth Street. The lodge's upkeep proved to be very expensive for the people of Royston but it did protect the surrounding stretch of country from 'Persons of base condition, and the scholars of Cambridge'. At the actual intersection of the two ancient highways there is a cave hewn out of the chalk, just below street level. A grille outside the bank on the corner of Melbourne Street is the only evidence from the street, but it is possible to go down into it through a doorway just across the road. A winding passage leads down to some 30 feet below the road, opening out to a bell shaped cave containing some weird but fascinating crude carvings depicting legendary and biblical scenes.

—Royston is at the foot of this high poor land; or rather in a dell, the open side of which looks towards the North. It is a common market town. Not mean, but having nothing of beauty about it; and having on it, on three of the sides out of the four, those very ugly things, common-fields, which have all the nakedness, without any of the smoothness, of Downs.

CHALKSCAPE AT REED

THE ROYAL HUNTING LODGE

ST. CHRISTOPHER, ROYSTON CAVE

Away from the town on the A505 lies the heath known as Therfield Heath. This is an area of rolling chalk downs. It is now public land and ancient burial mounds, which should not be confused with the surrounding golf bunkers, mark the top of the hill. The tenth hole has a view comparable with the ridge at Reed. This area must be one of the most walkable areas, with wonderful views from almost every angle and there are many wild flowers at the foot of the hills. Away to the north from near the 'one hill' can be seen the famous park surrounding Wimpole Hall.

Leaving Royston, the A10 bears away up to Cambridge and the Old North Road becomes the A14. We are now well into Cambridgeshire. (The county border runs through the centre of Royston.) Open land stretches away to the west and here I can only presume was the place that Cobbett described as, 'the most beautiful tract of fields that I ever saw'. The fields are now covered by the aerodrome which, together with some faceless barracks, now dominate the area. It is still 'a perfect level' though there are no longer any 'quick-set hedges'!

KING STREET, ROYSTON

THERFIELD HEATH

Huntingdon,
Tuesday morning, 22 Jan.

Immediately upon quitting Royston, you come along, for a considerable distance, with enclosed fields on the left and open common-fields on the right. Here the land is excellent. A dark, rich loam, free from stones, on chalk beneath at a great distance. The land appears, for a mile or two, to resemble that at and near Faversham in Kent, which I have before noticed. The fields on the left seem to have been enclosed by act of parliament; and they certainly are the most beautiful tract of *fields* that I ever saw. Their extent may be from ten to thirty acres each. Divided by quick-set hedges, exceedingly well planted and raised. The whole tract is nearly a perfect level. The cultivation neat, and the stubble heaps, such as remain out, giving proof of great crops of straw, while, on land with a chalk bottom, there is seldom any want of a proportionate quantity of grain.

EAST OF ROYSTON

Even here, however, I saw but few swedish turnips, and those not good. Nor did I see any wheat drilled; and observed, that, in many parts, the broad-cast sowing had been performed in a most careless manner, especially at about three miles from Royston, where some parts of the broad lands seemed to have had the seed flung along them with a shovel, while other parts contained only here and there a blade; or, at least, were so thinly supplied as to make it almost doubtful whether they had not been wholly missed. In some parts, the middles only of the ridges were sown thickly. This is shocking husbandry. A Norfolk or a Kentish farmer would have sowed a bushel and a half of seed to the acre here, and would have had a far better plant of wheat.—About four miles, I think it is, from Royston you come to the estate of Lord Hardwicke. You see the house at the end of an avenue about two miles long, which, however, wants the main thing, namely, fine and lofty trees. The soil here begins to be a very stiff loam at top; clay beneath for a considerable distance; and, in some places, beds of yellow gravel with very large stones mixed in it.

A BYGONE AGE

Cambridgeshire in Cobbett's time was considered to be one of the worst cultivated counties in England. Enclosure brought more efficient farming methods but The Enclosure Act took a long time to enforce. By 1847 all but six parishes had been enclosed; the last was Hildersham which was not enclosed until 1889, being one of the last in the country. The increased efficiency in agricultural methods created widespread unemployment amongst the labouring communities, which was one of Cobbett's major concerns. It also meant the cultivation of common and wasteland. The country poet John Clare wrote:

"And birds and trees and flowers without a name
All sighed when lawless law's enclosure came".

He was lamenting the disappearance of uncultivated land and the natural habitats of many wild species. What he did not live to see was the destruction of hedgerows in this century. This has become a far greater threat to wildlife, which at least had taken refuge in the network of hedges Enclosure had made necessary.

RECLAIMING WOODS IN THE 1850's

Bassingbourne, to the west of the road, has grown up from a few straggling farmhouses to flank the aerodrome. It now joins the village of Kneesworth on the opposite side of the road. In this area in particular you can see many 'clunch built' houses; clunch is a stone hewn from a ten foot seam of the Middle chalk, known locally as 'Melbourne Rock', which makes very fair building stone. Whaddon lies to the north of Kneesworth and its church is a prominent landmark from the road. The village is one of the few that flank the valley flats of the River Cam, here in its infancy. The river is sparsely lined with willows marking its path away to the east. The valley is, surprisingly, five miles wide at this point, providing fertile grey gault reminiscent of the Fens. I turned off the Ermine Street down a bumpy track marked 'Public Footpath to Whaddon Church', past a barn and up to the grand avenue of elms leading to Wimpole Hall. Originally this ran from the road in a double avenue, like a nave and aisle, one hundred yards wide and over two miles long, as an approach to the hall. It is likely that Cobbett would have been able to see the full length of the avenue as he passed along what is now the A14. More recently the area between the road and the footpath has been allowed to grow wild, and in the second World War the fifty acre thicket was used to conceal the bombers from the nearby aerodrome during their grounding for servicing and maintenance. The avenue now effectively begins at the farm track. Sadly it has suffered from the rampaging Dutch elm disease which has taken a terrible toll in East Anglia. Even before the disease high winds and storms had decimated the trees, most of which are very old. Cobbett was not impressed by elms and thought that this avenue, in particular, was a shabby show. He suggested planting ashes or oaks. Oak trees were a great favourite. Ironically 150 years later the soundness of his prejudices are well illustrated. The local farmer told me that as the elms died they had been replaced by ashes and oaks. At the time of writing the old elms are being uprooted

The land is generally cold; a great deal of draining is wanted and yet, the bottom is such as not to be favourable to the growth of the *oak*, of which sort I have not seen one *handsome* tree since I left London. A grove, such as I saw a Weston in Hertfordshire, would here, be a thing to attract the attention of all ranks and all ages. What, then, would they say, on beholding a wood of oaks, hickories, chestnuts, walnuts, locusts, gum-trees, and maples in America!—Lord Hardwicke's avenue appears to be lined with elms chiefly. They are shabby. He might have had *ash*; for the ash will grow *anywhere;* on sand, on gravel, on clay, on chalk, or in swamps. It is surprising that those who planted these rows of trees did not observe how well the ash grows here! In the hedge-rows, in the plantations, everywhere the ash is fine. The ash is the *hardiest* of all our large trees. Look at trees on any part of the sea coast. You will see them all even the firs, lean from the sea breeze, except the ash. You will see the oak *shaved up* on the side of the breeze. But the ash stands upright, as if in a warm woody dell. We have no tree that attains a greater height than the ash; and certainly none that equals it in beauty of leaf. It bears pruning better than any other tree. Its timber is one of the most useful; and as underwood and fire-wood it far exceeds all others of English growth. From the trees of an avenue like that of Lord Hardwicke a hundred pounds' worth of fuel might, if the trees were ash, be cut every year in prun-

THE AVENUE OF ELMS, WIMPOLE, JUNE 1976

THE AVENUE OF ELMS, WIMPOLE, DECEMBER 1976

DISEASED SECTIONS OF ELM

and burnt in this part of the avenue belonging to the National Trust, which runs from the intersection of the Cambridge Road, the A603, across up to the Hall.

Until recently the estate was owned by Rudyard Kipling's daughter, Mrs Bambridge, who when she died left the whole estate, over 2000 acres, to the National Trust. They have accepted it and it will be opened to the public in 1978. Until now, having been a private residence, it has long been shrouded in mystery. The locals make full use of the public footpath that runs through the grounds, right past the front of the house. This path dates back from the time when the estate was the centre of the local community. The village was on the estate and even the village church was built, as John Betjeman describes, 'in the Squire's Backyard'. So self-sufficient were the earls that the estate, then of 20,000 acres, had its own gasworks, timber yard, brewery, brickworks, blacksmith and wheelwright. Today little of these industries remain. Some traces of the brewery can be found at the back of the 'Hardwicke Arms', the estate pub on the main road which in Cobbett's day was known as 'The Tiger'. Further up the road the fine gates to the grounds stand opposite some almshouses. On the gates stand the crests of the Earls of Hardwicke, rampant on each pillar a stone lion and a unicorn.

ings necessary to preserve the health and beauty of the trees. Yet, on this same land, has his lordship planted many acres of larches and firs. These appear to have been planted about twelve years. If instead of these he had planted ash, four years from the seed bed and once removed; had cut them down within an inch of the ground the second year after planting; and had planted them at four feet apart, he would now have had about six thousand ash-poles, on an average twelve feet long, on each acre of land in his plantation; which, at three-halfpence each, would have been worth somewhere nearly forty pounds an acre. He might now have cut the poles, leaving about 600 to stand upon an acre to come to trees; and, while these were growing to timber, the underwood would, for poles, hoops, broomsticks, spars, rods, and faggots, have been worth twenty-five or thirty pounds an acre every ten years. Can beggarly stuff, like larches and firs, ever be profitable to this extent? Ash is timber, fit for the wheelwright, at the age of twenty years, or less. What can you do with a rotten fir thing at that age?—This estate of Lord Hardwicke appears to be very large. There is a part which is, apparently, in his own hands, as, indeed, the whole must soon be, unless he gives up all idea of rent, or unless he can *choack off* the fundholder or get again afloat on the sea of paper-money...

At an inn near Lord Hardwicke's I saw the finest parcel of dove-house pigeons I ever saw in my life.—Between this place

The footpath starts at the gates and winds through grassland dotted with some fine oaks and limes and some firs away on the northerly slope. I drove round to the other side of the grounds through New Wimpole village, built by the Earl, which stands on the Cambridge road, the A603. W. G. Hoskins, who describes Wimpole as 'the greatest mansion in the country', remarks that the 'estate village' was built in 1845, a period when such benevolent gestures were common. I followed a turning marked Old Wimpole to the left and soon came up to the old iron cattle gate. Walking under a fine line of hornbeam trees the stables were the first large buildings to come into view. The vast Hall was concealed by huge trees but, following the footpath, I was led round to the front of the house. I could see right to the end of the avenue originally laid out by Capability Brown. The house stood in its magnificence dominating a view that had altered little in the last 300 years. Wimpole is the epitome of 'a country seat'. The church, sheltered close under the east wing of the house, was obviously in everyday use, judging by the recent gravestones.

WIMPOLE HALL

THE FOOTPATH TO ELTISLEY

Back on the main road, and a few yards up from the almshouses, are some very old cottages. The crude thatch overhangs the irregular doors and windows set at various levels. On one of them I was very pleased to see the plaque of the Cambridge Cottage Preservation Society, a society formed with the intentions of preserving and modernising suitable cottages, thereby helping relieve local housing shortage and providing adequate amenities for tenants who prefer these cottage homes. The Society now owns more than forty cottages in ten Cambridgeshire villages and four in Essex. Most of their properties are of considerable rural interest and the standard of preservation is high.

Towards Caxton the road rises and falls through gentle arable slopes. The road was one of the first turnpikes in the country and there are still many of the original milestones visible on the west side of the road.

Caxton sits in a small dip in the fields. Almost the last house on the other side of the village used to be the courthouse but it was not built until the 1850's and has nothing to do with the famous gibbet that still stands by the intersection of the Ermine Street and the A45. Like many villages, Caxton becomes more interesting away from the High Street. The by-road running round the back and through the Firs farmyard is called St Peter's Street. I stood for half an hour one evening watching some house martins plucking up the courage to fly from the telegraph wires to their nest under the eaves of one of the farmyard buildings, knowing that I was watching them. A footpath leads off north-west towards Eltisley, and to one of the few coverts in the area, this one containing the ruins of an old Benedictine nunnery.

The Caxton gibbet now stands on the east side of the road. It originally stood on the west side and nearer to the village. It looks as if it could barely support a flag, let alone a man's carcass. Victims were actually never executed here but hung in Cambridge and their bodies then brought to this open and windy spot to dangle as warning to passers-by. Possibly the name of a lane a mile or so to the north has a connection. It is called Rogues Lane and runs round the back of the fields behind the next village. At the crossroads there is a pub, 'The Caxton Gibbet ', hardly the same pub that was there in Cobbett's day. Opposite is a garage called 'The Gibbet Garage'.

The open land rolls on uninterrupted except for a village called Papworth Everard, famous for the Papworth Chest Hospital. On its outskirts is 'Kisby's Hut', a pub with a history. It has been burnt down six times since 1735 when Samuel Kisby first started to sell beer to passengers from passing stage coaches. After the first fire he continued to sell from a hastily constructed horse barn.

Lattenbury Hill is the next high point and the road passes through a lovely copse of trees, many of which are beech. During the summer the road in the deep shade of these grand trees is illuminated every so often with wonderful bursts of light, shafting through gaps in the branches

THE CAXTON GIBBET

and Huntingdon is the village of Caxton, which very much resembles almost a village of the same size in *Picardy,* where the women drag harrows to harrow in the corn. Certainly this village resembles nothing English, except some of the rascally rotten boroughs in Cornwall and Devonshire, on which a just Providence seems to have entailed its curse. The land just about here does seem to be really bad. The face of the country is naked. The few scrubbed trees that now and then meet the eye, and even the quick-sets, are covered with a yellow moss. All is bleak and comfortless; and, just on the most dreary part of this most dreary scene, stands almost opportunely, *"Caxton Gibbet,"* tendering its friendly one arm to the passers-by. It has recently been fresh-painted, and written on in conspicuous characters, for the benefit, I suppose, of those who cannot exist under the thought of wheat at four shillings a bushel.
—Not far from this is a new house, which, the coachman says, belongs to a Mr. Cheer, who, if report speaks truly, is not, however, notwithstanding his name, guilty of the sin of making people either drunkards or gluttons. Certainly the spot, on which he has built his house, is one of the most ugly that I ever saw. Few spots have everything that you could wish to find; but this, according to my judgment, has everything that every man of ordinary taste would wish to avoid. The country changes but little till you get quite to Huntingdon. The land is generally quite open, or in large fields. Strong

overhead. On the other side the land becomes even flatter, with some neat farms on either side of the road. One final slope separated me from the wide valley of the Great Ouse. On the top is set a barn which, during the summer, appears to rise from a sea of corn. Down the hill, Godmanchester spread before me. This aspect is often obscured in mist and only the church tower gives any idea of the settlement. The town is ancient, the meeting point of four Roman roads. It has no market place and no High Street. It was a settlement of yeoman farmers and the fine architecture reflects this. Godmanchester is surrounded on all sides by fertile land and the river meadows. To the east is the largest meadow in the country, Port Holme. It was this that inspired Cobbett to write, 'by far the most beautiful meadows that ever I saw in my life '. The meadow, which covers over a square mile, is surrounded on three sides by the Great Ouse and on the fourth by the main railway line to Edinburgh. There are footpaths running across from three separate directions joining Godmanchester to Huntingdon and each to Brampton, the home of Samuel Pepys, on the far side. In high summer, during the hay making, there is nothing better than to walk over the meadow from river bank to river bank with the church spires, as Cobbett noted, raising their heads here and there. The outer loop of the river passes through Godmanchester. There is a wide pond fronted by a terrace of fine Georgian houses and the river flows under the famous 'willow-pattern' bridge by the side of the old town hall. It passes along the backs of some beautiful gardens with a few gazebos and eventually into the mill-pond. The

GODMANCHESTER

wheat-land, that wants a good deal of draining. Very few turnips of any sort are raised; and, of course, few sheep and cattle kept. Few trees, and those scrubbed. Few woods, and those small. Few hills, and those hardly worthy of the name. All which, when we see them, make us cease to wonder, that this country is so famous for *fox-hunting*. Such it has doubtless been, in all times, and to this circumstance Huntingdon, that is to say, Huntingdun, or Huntingdown, unquestionably owes its name; because *down* does not mean *unploughed* land, but open and *unsheltered* land, and the Saxon word is *dun*.—When you come down near to the town itself, the scene suddenly, totally, and most agreeably, changes. The *River Ouse* separates Godmanchester from Huntingdon, and there is, I think, no very great difference in the population of the two. Both together do not make up a population of more than about five thousand souls. Huntingdon is a slightly built town, compared with Lewes, for

THE OLD MILL POND, GODMANCHESTER

THE MILL STREAM

THE GREAT OUSE, HUNTINGDON

PORTHOLME MEADOW FROM BRAMPTON

O/S153

mill was destroyed many years ago but the mill-stream and the pond are surrounded by weeping willow trees. The river winds away out of sight from the mill-pond and follows the raised causeway, lined with lime trees, across the meadows to Huntingdon. Sadly, today, the Huntingdon bypass which has spared the town has laid waste the landscape. Instead of peaceful meadows and the quiet ripple of the river, there is a huge flyover and the constant roar of the internal combustion engine. However, the view of the meadows is incomparable from the height of the causeway, as is the view down river towards Houghton Mill from the old stone bridge, the original bridge over the Great Ouse. This was the crossing for Ermine Street, closely guarded by the Romans, and round which Godmanchester grew. Today the town has some beautiful houses as evidence of its former importance as a county town. Opposite All Saints Church is the Oliver Cromwell Museum, the building where Oliver Cromwell was educated; his birthplace was further up the street. The poet William Cowper also lived here; his house is now the offices of the local newspaper, 'The Hunts Post'. Of Huntingdon, Cowper wrote:"The longer I live here, the better I like the place and the people who belong to it. I am on very good terms with no less than four families, besides two or three old scrambling fellows like myself'. Of the river he wrote: 'It is the most agreeable circumstance in this part of the world. A noble stream to bathe in, and I shall make use of it three times a week having introduced myself to it first this morning '.

instance. The houses are not in general so high, nor made of such solid and costly materials. The shops are not so large and their contents not so costly. There is not a show of so much business and so much opulence. But Huntingdon is a very clean and nice place, contains many elegant houses, and the environs are beautiful. Above and below the bridge, under which the Ouse passes, are the most beautiful, and by far the most beautiful, meadows that I ever saw in my life. The meadows at Lewes, at Guildford, at Farnham, at Winchester, at Salisbury, at Exeter, at Gloucester, at Hereford, and even at Canterbury, are nothing, compared with those of Huntingdon in point of beauty. Here are no reeds, here is no sedge, no unevennesses of any sort. Here are *bowling-greens* of hundreds of acres in extent, with a river winding through them, full to the brink. *One* of these meadows is the *race-course*; and so pretty a spot, so level, so smooth, so green, and of such an extent I never saw, and never expected to see.

OLIVER CROMWELL MUSEUM

CHINESE BRIDGE, GODMANCHESTER

VIEWS ALONG RIVERBANK

Certainly the river has a great deal to do with the attraction of the place. A little path, known to fishermen, runs down the side of the north bank, going downstream from the bridge. It wanders through derelict gardens with roses and fruit trees and along the water's edge. On the opposite bank the meadows fold away to concealed boatsheds amongst the distant willows. Get lost down here, you'll never want to come back.

I am indebted to Colonel Donald Portway for the following riddle which he told me whilst I was a schoolboy in Cambridge:

Why is the Great Ouse like a flea?

Because it goes through Beds and Hunts and comes out in the Wash.

From the bridge you look across the valleys, first to the west and then to the east; the valleys terminate at the foot of rising ground, well set with trees, from amongst which church spires raise their heads here and there. I think it would be very difficult to find a more delightful spot than this in the world. To my fancy (and every one to his taste) the prospect from this bridge far surpasses that from Richmond Hill.—All that I have yet seen of Huntingdon I like exceedingly. It is one of those pretty, clean, unstenched, unconfined places that tend to lengthen life and make it happy.

THE RIVER OUSE

Journeyman's Notes

Journeyman's Notes

Journeyman's Notes

Selected Bibliography

Besides many local guidebooks and pamphlets, too numerous to mention, constant reference has been made to the relevant volumes of 'The Buildings of England' series, edited by Sir Nikolaus Pevsner and also 'The King's England' series, edited by Arthur Mee. A further selection of books is listed below:

Kensington to Uphusband:
'Portrait of Surrey' Basil E. Cracknell, Robert Hale 1970.
'Surrey Villages' Derek Pitt & Michael Shaw, Robert Hale 1971.
'Hampshire' Ralph Dutton, Batsford 1970.
'Hampshire & the Isle of Wight' A Temple Patterson, Batsford 1976.
Through Romney Marsh:
'Romney Marsh' Walter Murray, Robert Hale 1972.
'The Cinque Ports and Romney Marsh' Margaret Brentnall, John Gifford 1972.
'Kent Villages' Alan Bignell, Robert Hale 1975.
'The Companion Guide to the Coast of South-East England' John Seymour, Collins 1975.
'Kent' Roger Higham, Batsford 1974.
The Huntingdon Journal:
'London's Epping Forest' J. A. Brimble, Country Life 1950.
'Hertfordshire' W. Branch Johnson, Batsford 1970.
'A View into Cambridgeshire' Michael Rouse, Terence Dalton 1974.
'Cambridgeshire' E. A. R. Ennion, Robert Hale 1951.
'Fenland River' Rodney Tibbs, Terence Dalton 1969.

Index

*Numbers in italics indicate
illustrations or map references*